"I've known Karen Lafferty since the 19__ _____ _____ment was at its peak on the West Coast. But I didn't know the details of her story—until now. Her music, especially her classic 'Seek Ye First,' was a mainstay at Calvary Chapel in those days. She has made a notable impact around the world with her life and ministry. Karen's book, *Seek Ye First: The Karen Lafferty Story,* is a beautifully honest and compelling account of her personal growth and struggles. From a small New Mexico town to Southern California's beaches, from Amsterdam to sending out musicians as missionaries, Karen's journey is real and raw. I love a good autobiography, and this is a great one. Thank you, Karen, for sharing a backstage peek into your life while bringing encouragement to my own."

Skip Heitzig
Pastor of Calvary Church, Albuquerque, NM
Author of *The Bible from 30,000 Feet*

"Karen's book is like a Bible story—naked, honest, and straight-forward. Here is the story of someone who developed a deep desire to follow God despite a very mixed and sometimes difficult childhood. She had to butt heads with religion and abusive men on the way, but she carried on with a call that brought reality and hope to many and which we're sure still does. It reminds us of the words of Jesus: 'In this world, you will have trouble. But take heart! I have overcome the world.' We respect and honor Karen because of the realities of life about which she has written. She has exposed life situations that most of us would have left covered, except, perhaps, to tell a counselor. By revealing what went on between the stage and the private places of her life, she has shown us what life is often really all about."

David and Dale Garrett
Founders of Scripture in Song, New Zealand

"Stories can change lives, and the stories of ordinary people doing extraordinary things can change the world. *Seek Ye First: The Karen Lafferty Story* is the testimony of one such extraordinary person, the missionary pioneer, beloved mentor, and gifted songwriter Karen Lafferty, who composed one of the greatest Christian songs of the last fifty years, 'Seek Ye First.'

"Rarely can we look with such clarity into the life of a contemporary woman of God and see how God uses our frailty and brokenness. First, he moves us toward humble submission to Christ and then uses our gifts to further the purposes of his kingdom. If you are an artist or creative person, Karen's story will inspire you. It will show you how God makes use of our passions and talents when, even in our brokenness, we choose to follow Jesus' sacrificial path to serve others."

Rev. Dr. Byron Spradlin
President of Artists in Christian Testimony International,
Brentwood, TN

"I couldn't put this book down. Why? Because autobiography written in stark honesty is a rare gift. Are you artistic? Are you part of the emerging creative economy? How do you navigate a world in constant change? This book is your guide. The marketplace is changing, but true wisdom is timeless. Follow Karen, and you will make it."

John Dawson
President emeritus of Youth With A Mission

"I just read Karen Lafferty's book *Seek Ye First* in one sitting and was thrilled to watch over God's shoulder as Karen recounted her journey toward his call on her life. What became so clear to me were the stages of her journey as identified in Robert Clinton's book *The Making of a Leader*. From her 'sovereign foundations' in Alamogordo to her 'preset stage of convergence,' the ever-present Father continually spoke to Karen, watching and waiting for her. God's work of inner life development continues throughout our entire life but never hinders him from releasing us as his agents of blessing. Karen's humility, transparency, and openness throughout her story illustrate that truth. From a remote country town to the world and back again, Karen has more than forty years of teaching the world to worship God, who alone is worthy."

Tom Hallas
Elder of Youth With A Mission Asia-Pacific

"My initial meeting with Karen was on the road in 1971. Since then, I continue to be deeply impressed not only by Karen's voice, facility with guitar, and songwriting skills, but most of all, her walk with Jesus—it is genuine. Karen has always been a leader with a mission— to draw people to the love and saving grace of Jesus Christ. She shares her struggles and the experiences of a Christian troubadour forging into the uncharted territories of the early Jesus movement, led by the hand of God. She tells her compelling story with complete honesty and a rare humility not usually found in an autobiography. The language and presentation of the book are intelligent while accessible to a wide audience of readers. This book is a must-read for aspiring music missionaries and Christians in various fields of the arts."

Georgia Gene Berryhill, PhD
Bass player for The Surfaris
Adjunct professor of art history, University of Maryland-UMGC

"*Seek Ye First: The Karen Lafferty Story* is a book about overcoming not only abuses but failures and turning them into victories through Jesus. If you have struggled in your own life, this book will inspire you that there are answers out there to the hard questions of life."

Loren Cunningham
Founder of Youth With A Mission

"*Seek Ye First: The Karen Lafferty Story* tells how the 'Master Artist' takes a gifted young musician, despite past wounds and personal struggles, and calls her to reflect his truth and beauty to the nations. Karen's journey will inspire all who read it to trust God with their dreams and to serve him with their gifts."

Colin Harbinson
International director of StoneWorks: A Global Arts Initiative
Creator of *Toymaker & Son*
Former international dean of College of the Arts, University of the Nations

"What a page-turning memoir about how God grabbed a musician and sent her on a global mission to raise up an army of discipled 'musicianaries' armed with songs and a special Scripture chorus that would circle the planet! Unvarnished, gutsy, and brutally honest, Karen's journey demonstrates God's favor and his unrelenting, redeeming grace."

Frank Fortunato
Lifelong music missionary with Operation Mobilization

SEEK YE FIRST

SEEK YE FIRST

The Karen Lafferty Story

KAREN LAFFERTY & BECKY HEFTY

credo
house publishers

Published in the United States of America by Credo House Publishers,
a division of Credo Communications LLC, Grand Rapids, Michigan
credohousepublishers.com

ISBN: 978-1-62586-214-3

You may request permission by emailing *SeekYeFirstBook@gmail.com*.

Contact Karen Lafferty: *KarenLafferty.com/Seek-Ye-First-Book*

Cover and interior design and layout by Frank Gutbrod
Cover photo by Jennifer Bullock

To the wounded who are longing to be healed.

To the healers who have learned to be
the heart and hands of God.

To the musicians who are honest enough
to write and sing about these things.

Contents

Foreword

My husband, Jimmy, and I have loved Karen ever since she auditioned for our musical *Come Together* while standing in a phone booth in her bathing suit at the Corona Del Mar beach in California. She got the job, and it has been our privilege to know and work with this courageous visionary ever since. Karen's Musicians for Missions schools and her unceasing encouragement of the arts in evangelism have had a worldwide impact.

Seek Ye First: The Karen Lafferty Story is the achingly honest story of this beautiful, multitalented, conflicted woman.

Karen's muse was, and is, music, which captured her early and laid a world of possibilities at her feet. Her show business ambitions were more than just dreams; she was a natural. But God had designed her for something different, something with eternal possibilities that found its initial expression in the early Jesus movement.

How Karen is driven into God's arms to fulfill those possibilities is a story of struggle on many levels. There's the struggle of a woman with a big vision for ministry looking for a spiritual home, a covering for counsel and prayer. There are conflicts with leadership and bouts of disillusionment and adaptation. Karen's story is also one of hard truths about confusion in sexual identity brought about by abuse.

Those who want to serve God in purity must make desperately important decisions, yet they still sometimes fail. Those people *need* this story. It is a saga of restoration and grace, of getting up, getting a new hold on God, trying again—and triumphing. I believe many who suffer in silence will be encouraged and renewed by Karen's unflinching telling of her story.

May God bless this book and those who read it.

Jimmy and Carol Owens
Songwriters, authors

Preface

I remember the flowers in the fields that have gone away,
The flowers in the fields and the trees on the hill,
And I'm going back someday.

—"The Flowers in the Fields" by Karen Lafferty, © 1966 Karen Lafferty

I came from what folksinger Joni Mitchell described as "a searching generation." In her 1970 anthem "Woodstock," she expressed our search as a longing to "get ourselves back to the garden." We start this life in innocence, and over time, the world corrupts our way. That's why every generation longs for a place of restored innocence, where peace and beauty exist, and where relationships are uncomplicated—a place where we *really live.*

At age seventeen, I wrote "My Biggest Dreams," a song that recalls youth's fragrance and asks what my dreams will be at age eighty-four. Will I look back on my life and smile at dreams fulfilled? Will I shed tears for crushed dreams? And ultimately, will I be at peace with my life journey? I now have more than seventy years of perspective. Thanks to the grace of God in my life, I can say "Yes" to it all.

In the early '90s, Kingsway Publishing in the United Kingdom asked me to write a book about my life. They were interested in the story of how the Scripture chorus "Seek Ye First" came to be written. I was flattered and surprised they thought my story was worth publishing. I thought, *If someone could read my story and save themselves from making some of the stupid, hurtful mistakes I've made, I need to be as honest as I can and be an example of God's mercy and grace.* God's grace has been and still is my life's theme.

I tried to write the book but never could quite get it organized. So Kingsway and I gave up on it. I was disappointed in myself, yet I'm thankful. I had many more lessons to learn in life.

When I finally felt compelled to write an account of my life, I was still unsure I could do it. About that time, I learned that my friend Becky Hefty at Youth With A Mission (YWAM) Montana was getting her degree in creative writing. Becky is one of those people with whom I always feel at ease. I've shared a long history of music ministry with her and her late husband, Larry. I watched Becky win her battle against cancer and grieved with her when Larry lost his life to the same disease.

When Becky shared with me some poetry and personal thoughts about that experience, I felt the Lord prompt me to seek her help in writing my story. I knew I could speak freely about my sometimes painful journey and trust her to express my thoughts and feelings.

Becky accepted the challenge, and it has been a creative journey that has deepened our friendship and brought healing to both of us. She has spent hundreds of hours interviewing me, writing, and editing. I like to compare her to a good record producer who brings out the best in an artist while taking great pains to preserve the words as a pure expression of that artist. Thank you, Becky. I love your heart.

I believe whenever a follower of Jesus tells their story, it becomes a continuation of God's narrative. Like yours, dear reader, my story consists of real-life joys, sorrows, adventures, failures, and disappointments. In the Bible, God never sugarcoated the sins and failures of those he called to serve him. That's why I tried to be as honest as possible in telling my story. It is not about my accomplishments but about what God has accomplished in me.

A few of you will remember some of the events I've shared because you were part of them. I've shared these stories from my perspective, so they may differ from what you remember. Some of the stories are difficult and full of conflict, misunderstanding, or failure. But I sought to show *my* failures alone and how God's grace worked in the midst of them. Above all, these stories are about forgiveness, reconciliation, and healing.

I hope you will identify with some of my more difficult circumstances and receive his grace as I did. Healing comes through forgiveness, knowing "God causes all things to work together for good to those who love God, to those who are called according to His purpose" (Romans 8:28 NASB).

God wants us to live full and abundant lives. He has places he wants to take us and purposes he intends to fulfill in and through us if we ask, listen, obey, and follow. Though my story may resonate most with musicians and artists, the life lessons apply to all. God has a design for every life, and whatever successes I've had in long-term ministry in music and missions are because of him. He gets all the glory, honor, and praise!

I encourage you to write your own story, even if it's in journal form for your family. It will help you see God's grace in your life. I am hopefully wiser than I was before starting this book. I see God's dealings with and blessings toward me so much clearer, and I am grateful and humbled. I understand Jesus' words more than ever: "Seek ye first the kingdom of God, and his righteousness; and all these things shall be added unto you" (Matthew 6:33 KJV).

Karen Lafferty

Winter 2022

My Music — My Story

I am a singer/songwriter and storyteller. I talk about many of my songs throughout this book because they tell so much of my story. We have included QR codes at the end of the book so you can hear the songs I mention. You can also find all of my songs at KarenLafferty.com under the Discography section. Here is the QR code for my website.

KarenLafferty.com

CHAPTER 1

A Place to Call Home

Where else on earth does the sky look so blue,
The nights so clear, stars seem to sparkle like new.
God is the artist with beauty so rare,
He can paint a red sunset in New Mexico air.

—"New Mexico Song" by Karen Lafferty, from *Life Pages—Love of the Ages*
© Capitol Christian Music Group

Some say that in the high desert of New Mexico, the stars shine brighter than anyplace else on the earth. We four Lafferty kids thought so when we rolled out our sleeping bags under the night sky in the backyard of our Alamogordo home. How the stars sparkled and pulsed once the sun went down, taking its shades of fire with it! When the evening song of the crickets rose, I was convinced in my little girl's mind that those twinkling stars created the sweet music. I suppose I was born with music in my soul.

To a high-spirited girl like me, Alamogordo seemed like the best place any kid could grow up. It had cowboys and Indians, rockets and railroads, parades and rodeos, forested peaks and sugar-white dunes, and all the delicious color and spice of New Mexican culture.

I entered the world on February 29, 1948, straddling a time bridge between the past and future of Alamogordo. Until World War II, Alamogordo was mainly a cow town. But the White Sands Missile Range put our small community on the map in a whole new way. Space and military developments at the missile range and nearby Holloman Air Force Base shined a national spotlight on us. In 1961, the first spacecraft to orbit the earth carrying a living creature—a chimpanzee named Ham—earned our town the nickname "Rocket City."

Alamogordo also made Hollywood news. The nearby alkali flats had an otherworldly feel that attracted film crews shooting science fiction movies. They also made horror flicks, using magnified images of our desert horned toads for the monsters. My sister Fran and I hung around the motels in town, pestering the actors and actresses for autographs.

We Laffertys were as connected to the land as those "horny toads" by way of strong-minded ranchers and businessmen on both sides of my family line. In 1920, Sam and Satie Stout, my mom's parents, moved to Alamogordo from Wichita Falls, Texas. They had heard from friends that "everyone had a cherry tree or a peach or a pecan tree in their yard." They purchased the local ice plant and coal business. Later, they built an Olympic-size community swimming pool filled with the meltwater from the ice plant. My mom taught me how to swim and dive off a springboard at that same pool many years later.

Daddy's father, a gangly, colorful, redheaded cattleman known as Big Jim Lafferty, worked local ranches and later ran herds of horses and cattle down in Mexico. It was a lonely, isolated life there for his family. After one of Daddy's brothers nearly died from appendicitis, my Grandma Mettie moved the kids to Alamogordo within reach of schools and doctors. Daddy was about ten years old when his folks separated permanently.

Unlike his dad, my father, Walter Lafferty, was small in stature and had no interest in punching cattle. He stayed in Alamogordo and went to school while working three jobs to help care for his family. One of his jobs was at a local pharmacy. In 1935 (a year after eloping with my then seventeen-year-old mom), Daddy took the New Mexico Board of Pharmacy examination and passed. He was twenty-one years old and was the last person in New Mexico to earn a pharmacy license without a university degree.

I was the baby of my family, trailing my brother and two sisters. I was closest in age to my brainy and popular sister Fran, and I wanted to be just like her. My childhood memories reflect luxuries like a big house, a housekeeper, and vacations to Disneyland. But my brother Walter and oldest sister Satie say Daddy endured long, difficult years to reach the place of ease I took for granted.

After the Pearl Harbor attack, thousands of US military and their families descended on Alamogordo to find a shortage of houses and tough economic times. The townspeople, my folks included, opened their homes and hearts to them. The increased business overwhelmed all of the drug stores in town. Daddy worked from seven in the morning until eleven at night.

Many of the airmen and their families couldn't even afford basics, and Daddy refused to send them away empty-handed. Sometimes he even traded medicine for trinkets. He had a drawer full of stuff sick and desperate people had given him in exchange for precious medications. Daddy closed one fiscal year carrying a whopping $30,000 in outstanding debts—a massive amount of money in those days!

By the time I was ten, Daddy was a trusted professional and owned three pharmacies in Alamogordo. In 1956, he ran for city commissioner and won by a considerable margin—a testament to the town folks' high regard for him.

But Daddy was even more significant than that in my eyes. He was my hero.

In a photo taken at White Sands, he kneels alongside Fran. Both have scraped a pile of sand up and over their knees. Daddy's dark hair is slicked back and waved '50s-style. His broad black tie is tacked to his starched white shirt and tucked into dark-colored trousers. He's the picture of a businessman and a dad, at ease with each other in the same skin. Daddy was never too busy to come straight home from work and spend time with us.

My mom, who everyone called Ollie, was a notable figure in her own right in Alamogordo. She reminded me of Lucille Ball, a comic dynamo in a petite five-foot-two frame. Mom was ash-blonde but always wanted to be a redhead, so she dyed her hair strawberry blonde. Whatever she did, she was continually the leader of the pack and the life of the party.

Mom was fit, classy, and always dressed to kill, wearing beads and fancy coats and collars. She was equally comfortable on her knees, up to her elbows in garden dirt, or casting a fishing line from a boat. Mom sewed continually for herself and us kids and made outstanding costumes for herself and Daddy when they attended costume parties. Mom was also a fine musician. She grew up playing honky-tonk and ragtime piano for dances at her family's barn, which they turned into a dance hall, near the family swimming pool. She passed her love and gift of music down to me.

I remember seeing Mom reading her Bible in the mornings. She ingrained in us the importance of regular church attendance and made getting up on Sunday mornings an absolute pleasure. We awoke on church days to the smell of bacon frying. When we got to the table, hot homemade biscuits and fresh strawberries were waiting for us.

I don't doubt that Mom's faith was rooted in the example set by her mother, my Grandma Satie Stout. Grandma Stout had the kind of faith in God that wasn't just for Sundays. She wore her King James Bible out. Judging by the notes she kept on the many people she prayed for, it may be that she wore her knees out too. It was commonplace for Grandma Stout (who we affectionately called "Woo Woo") to gather all of us together to play music. Grandma led us on her musical saw (played with a bow) with Mom on piano, Uncle Pinky on harmonica, and me on guitar. She used her homemade songbook filled with old hymns.

In those days, all of my friends went to one of the churches in town. We prayed before sporting events and held baccalaureate services to encourage high school graduates to pursue God and virtuous endeavors in life. We even prayed together at school when we heard of President John F. Kennedy's assassination. I'm grateful for my parents, who raised me in the ways of the Lord and took me to church, and for a grandmother who was an ever-present reflection of God's grace. I'm also thankful for my upbringing in a community culture that respected the Lord.

When I set out on my musical journey as a young woman, writing songs about my beginnings—deeply rooted in faith—came naturally. I wrote "Grandma Stout" as a tribute to my grandmother's healthy prayer life and unwavering love for God. "Testimony" recalled the day I surrendered to Jesus, surrounded by family and friends at the altar of my home church. And "New Mexico Song" voiced my deep gratitude for this beautiful land and its people.

To this day, I love small-town life and its strong sense of family and community. Faith, family, hometown values, and the beauty and culture of New Mexico are woven together in a strong cord. That cord has kept me firmly tied to my beliefs and ideals no matter how far away from Alamogordo or New Mexico I've lived and traveled. These things define home for me, and home is where my story begins.

CHAPTER 2

Leap Year

In its heyday, the local drugstore embodied small-town
American culture. It was much more than a place to buy
medicine or material goods. It was a social outlet that drew
neighbors together around tables or the iconic soda fountain lined
with shiny metal stools. My first job was as a soda jerk, making
ice cream sundaes, shakes, and malts for locals at our downtown
drugstore. Mom, Fran, our housekeeper, Sarah, and I also made
the delicious tuna, chicken, egg salad, ham, and cheese spread
sandwiches our customers loved.

Daddy worked the pharmacy. Mom, an exceptional
businesswoman, put in hours in the vault at the main store handling
all three of our pharmacies' bookwork. My siblings and I worked the
soda fountains and did seasonal jobs. We were expected to respond
to our customers with a "yes ma'am" or "no sir" and address our

elders as mister, miss, or missus. Our customers included Native Americans from the Mescalero Apache reservation, cowboys, military families, Mexicans, and ordinary townsfolk. It seemed to me that Daddy knew all of them personally.

Unlike my mom, work was Daddy's religion. He worked long hours seven days a week. It took a crisis involving my brother Walter to bring him to the Lord.

When Walter was eleven years old, he contracted bulbar poliomyelitis, a polio form that affects the throat and lungs. Mom and Daddy feared for Walter's life after he ran a fever of 107 degrees for several days. They rushed him to Carrie Tingley Hospital in the town of Truth or Consequences. When they arrived, there were already multiple beds lining the hallways, occupied by dying children.

"Put him over there," a tired doctor told them when they rushed in with Walter. After examining him, the doctor turned to them and said sadly, "Don't bother praying. Your son is too far gone to save."

Mom and Daddy were stunned.

"Surely there's something you can do, something we can try?" Daddy said. "Can't you put him in that new iron lung? We have nothing to lose. Please, at least *try* to save my son!"

"There are so many here also in need," the doctor said, motioning toward the dying children. "And there is no guarantee it will work for your son. I'm sorry."

"Please," Daddy begged again, "please try. It's our only hope." Miraculously, the doctor relented, and they placed Walter in an iron lung.

Walter lay in a coma for days. A local pastor came in and prayed for him. My daddy kept vigil, begging, "Please God, save my boy!"

And God did.

Walter regained consciousness, opening his eyes and squinting above his head at the distorted reflections of nurses in white uniforms moving past the lung's silver casing. "I thought I had died," he later told us, "and that the reflections I saw were angels. And I remember being thirsty."

Sensing moisture in the tube, Walter somehow wiggled his head out of the lung's collar. He made his way into the interior of the tube in search of a drink, disappearing from view. The nurses panicked when they noticed he was gone, and they quickly opened the iron lung. He screamed, and they screamed. "It was quite a scene!" Walter said.

Mom arrived after the nurses got Walter calmed down and repositioned in the lung.

"Mom," he whispered. "Mom." Thrilled that he was conscious and communicating, she put her ear close to his lips, trying to make out his hoarse whisper.

"Mom, I want a peanut butter sandwich." Walter's favorite food!

Mom and Daddy cried with relief. They knew then he would pull through.

Walter survived and went on to play football. My daddy received Jesus and began attending church. However, as a city official and wealthy businessman, Daddy came under constant pressure to give to the church financially. He stopped going, except for special occasions. The rest of us continued to attend regularly, my mother taking on the role of spiritual mentor in our lives.

Even though Daddy stopped coming to church with us, I was still proud of him. I wanted his approval for all the things that mattered to me. In March of 1957, I hit my first spiritual milestone. I made the heartfelt decision to go forward, receive the Lord, and get baptized. I yearned for my daddy to watch me take that step forward. I waited for Easter Sunday, knowing he would be there. That day, I proudly walked up the aisle in a beautiful dress with a satin bow, keenly aware of Daddy's eyes on me.

The Lafferty family appeared to be a success by all social and economic standards. Outwardly, we must have looked like the perfect American family to our community. But inwardly, we faced struggles that were becoming increasingly difficult to hide.

My sister Satie got pregnant and married at the age of fifteen. Mom and Daddy gave her the vital support she needed while doing their best to deal with the gossip and disapproval it caused. (Even though she was soon divorced, Satie later remarried. She went on to become a wonderful wife in a sixty-year marriage, a beloved mother, grandmother, great-grandmother, and a very warmhearted and accomplished woman.)

Walter was away at college and began drinking more. He sometimes arrived home drunk when he came back during breaks. While he didn't drink all the time, Walter seemed to become a different person whenever he drank until he was drunk. On one occasion, I awoke to find him boozed up and in my bed, his hands moving all over my body. I screamed, and my folks rushed in and pulled him away. I assume they dealt severely with him, but it was not the last time I endured his drunken advances. Those college homecomings caused me to fear for the first time.

There was little or no open discussion about intimacy, sex, and sexual attraction in that era. I grew up with a significant gap in my understanding of these things. Mom's only words about anything of a sexual nature were cryptic warnings delivered during my teenage years. They were probably rooted in having had to walk Satie through her pregnancy and marriage. I was clueless about recognizing and dealing with inappropriate sexual advances (and later, my sexual attractions).

I was also unprepared to deal with the drinking problem developing in our family. Our inability to constructively overcome this issue would become the source of years of pain and confusion for me.

My folks made the rounds of conventions, parties, service clubs, and community events as successful business people. They both drank and smoked socially in those settings. But unbeknownst to his associates, Daddy was quietly struggling with a drinking habit, slipping from acceptable levels of social drinking into the well-kept secret of private excess. We were contending with it daily at home. I can only guess how the stresses of work, family, and civic duty moved him to take refuge in alcohol. Unfortunately, our area had no programs for those suffering from alcoholism. My father didn't have a friend he trusted enough to help him.

Daddy was never abusive when he drank. When he was on a binge, he would sit in front of the television after we kids had gone to bed and drink himself into a stupor. Mom was not quiet about her feelings, and she felt justified in confronting the man she loved to get him to change. Fran and I learned what we knew of the problem from listening to their frequent arguments. Once we were in bed, Mom would launch into an emotional frenzy we could not help but overhear. Since Satie and Walter had moved away, we would huddle in our bedroom and plead with God to help our daddy stop drinking.

Sometimes Fran and I would sneak down the hall near the kitchen door to hear what they were saying. Most nights, we sat there, whimpering and crying in our helplessness. But during one explosive argument, Fran and I mustered all our courage and stepped into the kitchen. Daddy looked drunk and weary. His head hung low on his chest after enduring another of our mother's outbursts.

Fran cried, "We're worried about you, Daddy. Please, stop drinking!"

He looked sorrowfully at us but didn't say a word. I think he understood he needed to stop, but he was trapped in the depths of something we couldn't understand. No amount of our wishing would make the problem go away or keep his secret from eventual discovery.

After an uncomfortable silence, he finally spoke. "Looks like everybody's ag'n' me." The sadness in his voice broke my heart. *How could we convince him that we were* for *him and only wanted him to get through this, whatever it might take? Why couldn't he choose to stop?*

One summer morning, Daddy and I were home alone, and I pounced on the opportunity. I'd been watching for a time to tell him myself how much I wanted him to stop. I did all the talking, venting my frustrations.

"Daddy," I sobbed, "you *need* to stop drinking! It isn't good for Mom and us! I'm going to help you stop!" In my worked up, childish grief, I took the reins into my own hands and went straight for the alcohol under the sink, grabbing whatever I could find there. I pried the corks out of the bottles one by one and poured the expensive liquor down the sink as he stood by and watched. He made no move to stop me. It must have been horrible for him to see his ten-year-old daughter bent over the sink, weeping, with the smell of alcohol filling the kitchen. When I couldn't pry the cork out of one bottle, he took it gently, removed the cork himself, and handed the bottle back to me to drain.

Daddy's drinking did not end that morning. What it would take for my daddy to quit was beyond my youthful comprehension. Had I known how high his deliverance price would be, I would not have been so bold.

February 29, 1960, was supposed to be a special day. Even though I was only turning three as a leap-year baby, I was eager to celebrate my twelve years by having a party on the *actual* date once again. My head was buzzing with plans. But all of that changed on the night of February 17.

Our house was quieter than usual that evening. Mom was puttering with something in the kitchen. Daddy joined Fran and me for a game of marbles in the living room before sending us to bed. The colorful cat's-eyes, steelies, and shooters flashed and clacked as we girls laughed and played, content to be in the center of Daddy's universe. When he hugged and kissed us good night, I pressed my face into the warmth of his starched white shirt. I had never felt more secure in the strength of his arms.

Much later, I was frightened awake by hysterical wailing. A figure materialized in my bedroom—my mother's sister Nell.

"Karen," she choked, barely in control of herself, "your dad has been killed in a car accident." Sharp images of our game of marbles and the lingering warmth of his embrace, only hours old, flashed through my mind. Dead? *Dead?*

Within moments, Fran and I were in the kitchen with Nell and Mom, crying and trying to make sense of it all. *Are you sure? Couldn't they get him to the hospital? Maybe it's someone else? Dead instantly?* No matter how hard we tried, the reality of it wouldn't sink in.

Walt Mullins, Alamogordo's mortician and friend of our family, called Nell and my Uncle Herbert with the news first. He didn't want Mom to be alone when word reached her. The sheriff's deputies told them that Daddy had fallen asleep at the wheel or hit black ice somewhere between Alamogordo and Ruidoso. His car careened off the road and hit a tree. The impact snapped his neck.

Daddy had been drinking again and was more than likely drunk. He and Mom had argued. He may have left the house of his own accord, or she may have thrown him out. As an act of kindness, the authorities didn't mention he had been drinking to the public, mercifully maintaining Walter Lafferty's reputation in the community.

Daddy's death sent shock waves through Alamogordo. Condolences and mounds of flowers poured in. Mayor Charles

Sutton said: "I don't know when I've been so shocked. I've known Walter practically all of his life. He was one of the finest commissioners a fellow could serve with. The death of Walter Lafferty is a tragedy."

The mortuary kept its doors open the entire night before Daddy's funeral to accommodate the long line of mourners, many of whom were the community's most impoverished. They came from miles around to say goodbye.

My sister Satie later told me of meeting a janitor at the bank where she worked. When he learned that she was the daughter of Walter Lafferty, his eyes filled with tears. "When I came to this town," he explained, "I had no money, and my wife was very sick. Mr. Lafferty gave her medicine that saved her life." It was a story familiar to any number of Alamogordo's citizens.

I cried for days after his death. I couldn't imagine what life was going to be like without Daddy in it. And I was angry because I knew he had been drinking before the crash. How could he do this to us? How could he desert us like this? *Who was going to take care of me now?*

In the days and weeks that followed, I often went to my bedroom alone and called out to God for comfort and understanding. But the pain continued, leading to bitterness and unforgiveness. Only my faithful Father in heaven could restore what I lost when my beloved earthly father left me.

CHAPTER 3

Firm Foundation

"Life doesn't come with a manual; it comes with a mother."

—Author unknown

Mom was suddenly a widow, single mother, provider, and boss of a three-store corporation. Capable as she was, this was still an immense load on her small shoulders. Mom's faith, self-discipline, high work standards, and parental care kept life on track for our grieving family in the months following Daddy's death.

No doubt Fran and I added to her burden. We wanted to please Mom, but as emotional, headstrong teen girls, we often challenged her. It's incredible to me how much strength and patience she showed, propelling us through those hard days. Mom never seemed to lose perspective. She kept us working hard at home, school, and the pharmacy—to keep us moving forward instead of sinking into sadness. It would be a long time before I understood the scope of her strength and unselfishness and how it shaped who I am today. At the time, however, I could only see things through my heartaches and hormones.

At fourteen years of age, I thought I was pretty mature. Enough, at least, to date a boy who was not only a couple of years older than I was but who had a Caucasian mother and a Mexican father. In an era when racial mixing was frowned upon, Mom didn't approve.

"I have a date," I informed Mom one evening as she was getting supper ready.

"Oh? Who with?" she asked.

"Fred Lopez," I said carefully. "He's a senior at school." Mom flicked a glance at me. Her eyebrows arched almost imperceptibly. I felt the heat of argument rise in my chest and color my face.

"Well, Karen, I think there are other guys out there who are more your type," she replied calmly. Her answer was indirect but still pointed.

"He's a nice guy, Mom," I explained. "All my friends think so too."

"It's not what your friends think, Karen. It's what I think."

"But Mom," I reasoned. "Is it just that you don't want me to go out with someone who is half Mexican? I think Daddy would have let me. You know he had lots of Mexican friends."

"Karen, I just think Fred is too old for you. Please tell him I said no."

My disappointment over that exchange simmered for the next couple of weeks. One Friday night, I found myself home alone and grounded. Mom had gone out for the evening, and Fran was hanging out with friends at the local teen center. I was angry and decided to get drunk, perhaps to get back at Mom over what I saw as injustice.

I headed for the alcohol still hidden under the kitchen sink.

I was clueless about how to mix drinks, so I tried mixing gin and grape juice. It was awful. Then I tried the whiskey. I hated the taste of it but kept drinking until I was drunk. Next, I chose to do something that made no sense. I took a razor and started cutting the tops of my arms. Where the idea came from, I don't know. I wasn't suicidal, just driven by emotions and drink.

I wanted my friends to feel sorry for me, so I started calling them. I got sick and began throwing up while sitting in the hallway. Fran came home first and found me covered in vomit, so she cleaned me up and got me into bed before Mom returned.

When I awoke the following morning, I thought it was 9:30, and I knew I was late for my job at our drugstore. *Surely,* I thought, *Mom must know what I did and is letting me sleep it off. She must be so mad at me. Maybe if I confess what I did, she will go easier on me.* I got up and went to tell her what had happened.

Mom was still in her bedroom—up, dressed, bed made. It turned out to be only 7:30 in the morning. I owned up to what I had done, and the woman who always had something to say was unexpectedly silent. She just looked at me, slapped me across the face for the first time, and then sat down on her bed and started sobbing.

Whether because of the silence, the look, or the slap, something clicked inside me. I could only think: *Maybe Mom thinks I'm going to turn out like Daddy. She already carries such a load as a single mom, and here I am, adding to it.* I decided that morning I loved Mom too much to shame or embarrass her ever again. It was a painful lesson in love and grace, which would one day help me understand how unconditionally God loved me.

At age forty-three, it was understandable that Mom might want to remarry. But, to our surprise, she began seeing Paul Brown, the pharmacist at our Hospital Pharmacy. We'd grown up around the man, and neither Fran nor I cared for him. Although he was handsome, charming, and sophisticated in his way, he was not approachable like our daddy. We regarded Paul as both a threat and an unacceptable replacement.

When he and Mom started dating, I was irritated with pretending to be nice to someone I found so disagreeable. Then, as happens in a small town, people started gossiping. I was furious when my neighborhood friends began circulating the rumor that Mom was sleeping with Paul—an idea that undoubtedly came from their parents. I immediately ran to find Mom and delivered my preadolescent demand.

"Mom! You have to stop seeing Paul!" I blurted out. After letting me pour out my heart and shed my tears, she took me by the hand and sat me down.

"We need to talk about this, Karen," she said. "Paul and I have only been seeing each other. There is nothing physical going on. But you need to know that we *have* been talking about getting married." Mom spoke gently and evenly without scolding me; she wanted me to understand. I knew it had been hard for her since Daddy died. She wanted to remarry, but I couldn't swallow the prospect of *that* man in *our* family.

"I will *never* call him Daddy," I vowed.

Paul married my mother in 1962, just two years after Daddy's
death.

Once Paul was a permanent fixture in our household, Fran
and I had frequent run-ins with him, even over small things. He
didn't seem to know how to love or relate to us beyond telling
us how we could be doing something better. I never received any
personal affirmation from him.

Knowledgeable and well-read, Paul was a proud man, and he
loved playing the devil's advocate in family discussions. As strong-
minded as I was, I had a hard time learning *not* to argue with him.
The Lafferty's had always been a speak-your-mind family when
planning events or working things through. We were able to hear
and respect each other's opinions. But it didn't work that way once
Paul inserted himself into our family's process.

Paul professed to be a believer and considered himself an
authority on the Bible. Yet, he said Christians were "narrow-
minded." What he thought of my mother's faith, I don't know.
His dirty jokes and inappropriate innuendos convinced me that
he didn't have a sincere faith.

Paul had an adopted son named Jerry from a previous
marriage who was a year younger than I. Fran and I knew him
from school and our parents' social connections. We were aware
that Jerry was living with an emotionally needy mother who had
no idea how to parent him. Mom agreed to have Jerry come live
with us and included Fran and me in the family discussion. Even
though we felt unsure about having a brother added into the mix,

we could see that having Jerry live with us would be much better for him. We were glad to welcome him for that reason. True to form, Mom showered Jerry with motherly love in the same way she did with us once he became part of our family.

One of the ways Mom showed her love was by encouraging our dreams. When I was just six years old, she saw I had a passion for music. All my siblings had taken piano lessons, and all dropped out. I was different. I begged her for music lessons, and once she understood I was serious, she signed me up, kicking off a lifetime of music for me.

I spent many childhood hours in my room playing and listening to songs. Mom encouraged my growing passion and rewarded me for every show of diligence. I began playing saxophone at age nine, ukulele at age ten, guitar at age twelve, and oboe at age fourteen. Mom bought me a high-quality Selmer sax and a Rigoutat oboe when I was in junior high, and I still own and use them today. She bought me a simple Stella guitar and paid for two lessons when I expressed interest in learning guitar. I learned to play two songs—"Let the Rest of the World Go By" and "Tumbling Tumbleweeds"—so I could accompany her quartet at a country club luncheon in Alamogordo. That was the first time I performed publicly. It was exciting except for the moment at lunch when a waitress accidentally poured gravy down the back of my cowgirl outfit.

Perhaps Mom's single most significant contribution to my future as a musician came when I was sixteen years old. At the time, I was making my first 45 rpm vinyl record at Yucca Studios in Alamogordo. I was playing a borrowed 000-18 Martin guitar and had never used such a fine instrument. Mom must have noticed my joy because she bought me that superb guitar. For the next fifteen years, Luther (named after Martin Luther) was my constant sidekick in performing and songwriting.

I always felt that Mom wanted to be a musical performer and lived that out through my adventures. She was my unceasing encourager and kept a scrapbook of all my music performances, beginning with my first piano recital. She was always my biggest fan.

I loved attending summer music camps hosted by the universities in New Mexico during my high school years. While the camps were fun, they were also intense, stretching my musical skills. I became friends with gifted musicians from other towns, and being around them made me want to be part of a band or orchestra.

I hauled my guitar on numerous bus trips, playing at small concerts and hootenannies. I sang folk songs such as Bob Dylan's "Blowin' in the Wind" and Peter, Paul and Mary's "If I Had a Hammer." I sang justice songs like "We Shall Overcome," born of the civil rights movement, and antiwar music like "Where Have All the Flowers Gone?" and "One Tin Soldier." I saw myself in well-known female artists like Carole King, Anne Murray, Joan Baez, Judy Collins, and Joni Mitchell.

I formed a girl's trio called the Sundowners with my friends Annette Zimmerman and Bobbye Buttram. We sang the latest folk hits, experimenting with harmonies. I listened for hours to Peter, Paul and Mary's music and slowly learned the Travis picking method from Paul Stookey. It's one of the primary techniques I still use to play guitar today. I learned a whole new style from James Taylor: hammer-ons and pull-offs. Joni Mitchell's music introduced me to alternate tunings in "Big Yellow Taxi," and I picked up the drop D technique from John Denver. I also incorporated some of the Latin flavors of Sérgio Mendes & Brasil '66.

During high school, I hung out a lot with Jim from our church youth group. Jim was a get-it-done kind of person, like me, self-confident, polite, and liked by everyone at school. He didn't think that believing in God and going to church was a "sissy" thing. When he came to the house to pick me up for dates, Paul's mom would say, "Hey Karen, Mr. Prayer Meeting is here to get you!" I was flattered that Jim seemed to like spending time with me. We were genuinely good friends. I saw Jim as the guy I might marry after we both finished college.

Graduating from high school in 1966, I headed for Eastern New Mexico University in Portales to study music education. I was launching out at a time when the country was seething with racial unrest, antiwar sentiments, and the potent cultural elixir of sex, drugs, and rock and roll. However, I was still a clean-cut and optimistic hometown girl. I had a solid music foundation, a strong work ethic, a fundamental spiritual foundation, and all the self-confidence my mom had instilled in me. And I had a good relationship with a steady guy.

CHAPTER 4

Bitter and Sweet:
The Long Road of Learning

Been down to Australia, lived in New Mexico,
Seen the Arctic midnight sun, I've watched the rivers flow.
Though I've traveled places, seen many faces,
Not a thing on earth or above,
No, nothing can separate me from God's love.

—"Nothing Can Separate" by Karen Lafferty, from *Sweet Communion*
© Capitol Christian Music Group

I wanted to become a band instructor or choir director for two reasons. First, I needed a backup if my then-budding ambitions to be an entertainer fell through. Second, my mom always encouraged me to use my musical abilities to inspire others. I got a solid background in music and education at ENMU, thanks to professors like Dr. George Umberson. His passion for directing music and his wonderful sense of humor inspired my learning in music and theory. He also opened the door to performing in classical music recitals, pop, and Broadway variety shows. Soon I was hooked on performing.

The university was a great place to meet musicians and form bands. I kicked off my freshman year as part of a folk trio called The Joyful Noise. By my sophomore and junior years, I'd graduated to singing jazz and playing sax in a lounge band called The Chrystal Pavilion. There, thanks to the band's professional drummer, I learned the art of playing hand percussion instruments.

But the music of the day was psychedelic rock, and by the end of my junior year, I was playing in a rock band. My bandmates immersed themselves in the hippie lifestyle, dressing like flower children, espousing peace and love, and blasting loud rock and roll music. I played the part by donning round wire-rim glasses and fringed, paisley outfits. However, I didn't entirely fit the image because I wouldn't buy into the hippie movement's drugs and promiscuity.

We put all of the money from our first few gigs into buying a sound system to launch the band. I owned a 1969 Plymouth Satellite at the time—my hippie-mobile, complete with a "mod" flowery vinyl top and matching upholstery. I agreed to use it for our travels and pulling our equipment trailer. We were a five-member band with vocals, drums, bass, electric guitar, and keyboards. We traveled with a Hammond B3 organ and a Rhodes electric piano, both of which were state-of-the-art at the time. I was the sole girl in the band. I tried to mimic rock divas like Janice Joplin and Grace Slick—not a good practice for a vocal major. Since no self-respecting rock band at that time traveled without a psychedelic light show, we created one. We used black lights, projecting light through a transparent casserole dish filled with water and colored oil. The movement of the oil and water generated images that looked like amoebas surging onstage.

We had no relational problems as a band until my senior year when we divvied up the equipment before heading in different directions. The guys got into a heated debate about who would get what sound equipment. I didn't want any part of the argument. But since I had done my share to help make the band happen, I plucked up the courage to ask, "Hey guys, do I get something out of this? I was part of the band too." They looked at me awkwardly, as if it hadn't occurred to them that I deserved something also. They finally split it all between themselves and handed me a single microphone. That was the end of their "love your brother" hippie mantra. They made no effort to be fair or to account for the use of my car and money. They greedily grabbed up the equipment and split. That experience left me thoroughly disillusioned with the hippie philosophy.

One of my most significant music opportunities at ENMU came in the summer of 1968. The university was doing a USO musical extravaganza directed by Dr. Umberson, whom we affectionately called "Coach." I auditioned for the tour. They accepted me as part of the fourteen-member song and dance troupe scheduled to entertain at US military bases in Greenland, Iceland, and Canada, with a short side trip to England tacked on for fun.

The military flew us in a cargo plane to Thule, Greenland, and housed us in army barracks. We were transported to Artic performance locations by helicopter and issued oversized, Eskimo-style army parkas to keep us warm.

The servicemen at the US base in Thule manned the Ballistic Missile Early Warning System (BMEWS), which monitored Russia during the Cold War. The area is dark half the year and as lonely as the moon. Depression and alcoholism were common problems, so the men were only rotated in for short tours. Shows such as ours boosted morale and provided a connection to the outside world.

Our song and dance performance consisted of show tunes, patriotic music, standards, pop, and folk songs using guitars, a stripped-down drum set played by Coach, and if available, a piano. For our finale, the gals wore short chiffon dresses and the guys wore tuxes, giving our show a touch of class. We sang "The Impossible Dream" and "The Battle Hymn of the Republic" for a wholesome, stirring ending. The men loved it. At one of the more remote locations, we performed in a small mess hall. We exited toward the kitchen after the finale. Suddenly, the first performer in our line tripped on a rubber mat and went down. We all fell with him into a comical heap of bodies. The men roared with laughter. Embarrassed as we were, we certainly had done well as entertainment!

The best result of the tour was the long bond of friendship forged amongst our troupe members and the feeling that we had done something meaningful. By the time we headed back to the States, I knew I wanted to keep performing in front of live audiences. My thirst for travel and performance possibilities seemed unquenchable.

I discovered I could make decent money and gain performance experience by entertaining in restaurants and bars. I took entertainment jobs at nearby Cannon Air Force Base, Ruidoso, and Santa Fe. My mom, forever the manager, was also encouraging me to enter talent shows and pageants. I won the Miss Grain Sorghum beauty pageant in Demit, Texas (I didn't even know what grain sorghum was, so I had to look it up first), which launched me into guitar-picking performances at state and county fairs around Texas and New Mexico. I entered and won the Miss Central New Mexico Pageant, which placed me in the lineup for the Miss New Mexico Pageant scheduled for the summer of 1971. I also tied for first place in a talent show with a band called The Latinos. Our prize was opening for legendary comedian Bob Hope at The Pit, a sports arena in Albuquerque.

After the show at The Pit, a woman approached me to express interest in managing me. I was blown away and wondered, *Could this be the door to the "big time" for me?* I made a demo of my best songs for her, but at the time, it appeared that nothing came of it.

I had begun weaving myself into the university's social fabric early on when I pledged the Zeta Tau Alpha Sorority (ZTA). The Little Sisters of Minerva, the sisters component of my stepbrother's fraternity, Sigma Alpha Epsilon (SAE), invited me to join. I was one of the resident "folksingers" for these social organizations and other campus functions, which provided many music performance opportunities.

I liked what ZTA stood for; their campus and community service and their sorority rituals seemed worthy and Christian-based to me at the time. Once I became a sorority member, they elected me to the committee that dealt with the discipline of any sister who crossed the sorority's stated line of good conduct. However, I served with an increasing sense of guilt because I sometimes came close to crossing that line myself. I was moving away from the Lord as I pursued the excitement and "freedom" of campus social life.

One day, one of my sorority sisters pulled me aside to deliver some news.

"Hey, Karen. Just thought you should know that your boyfriend, Jim, has, well, he's pinned a girl here at ENMU."

I turned to look at her, astonished. "Jim? That can't be. He's not like that. He would have told me."

"Well," she said. "It's pretty common knowledge around campus. I'm sorry to be the one to break it to you. I just thought you should know."

It was a punch in the gut. Jim was dating another girl on *my* campus, right under my nose! Worse, everyone but me seemed to know about it.

I had let myself believe that Jim was serious enough about me to marry. Jim and I were still spending time together, even though our schools were in different towns. He even invited me to his campus once and took me out to spend time with him in a romantic setting. Jim was Mr. Charming. I could have sworn he was courting me. But pinning a girl—another girl—was practically the same thing as getting engaged. *Why didn't he tell me?*

I confronted him. "Jim! I heard you're dating another girl, right here on my campus!"

His gaze slid away from mine. "Yes," he admitted. "That's true."

"And you *pinned* her?"

"Yes, Karen. I did."

"But why? Why didn't you tell me? How could you lead me on like that?"

"Honestly, Karen, I just didn't know how to tell you," he said. "And I didn't want to hurt your feelings."

"So you thought I wouldn't find out? How long were you going to keep it from me? What a coward!" It became one more reason for me to believe that men were liars and abusers and were not trustworthy. One more reason to think men didn't care about me.

In a sorority dorm, young women live in tight quarters—hanging out, sharing bathrooms, moving between each other's rooms, piling on each other's beds, acting silly, and sometimes, carrying on physically. It can be fertile ground for budding same-sex attractions, which proved to be the case for me. Homosexuality was not socially acceptable or condoned by the sorority in the late 1960s. Yet it was still possible for one thing to lead to another, even in a place where we were seldom, if ever, alone. I'd had crushes on girls as well as guys since junior high, but I had resisted the former. Now, being burned in my relationship with Jim didn't help matters.

After I'd moved into a place of my own in my senior year, I entered into a brief same-sex attachment. It ended badly. I existed in a tearful tug-of-war between my emotional connection in that relationship and my conscience telling me that it was inappropriate. My conscience was still sensitive enough to keep me in a place of wrestling with this issue before the Lord.

I wasn't able to build a lasting, trusting relationship with a man throughout my university years. Yet, it was easy to find the nurture and attention I desired from women. It was a bitter, painful place to be. But even though I felt trapped in my sin and confusion at the time, my heavenly Father had taken heed of my tears and anguished prayers.

CHAPTER 5

The Good, the Bad, and the Way Back

I've tried, and I've failed, and I've won.
I've fallen then got up to run.
But when it's been all said and done,
You sure have been good to me.

—"You Sure Have Been Good to Me" by Bill Batstone, as recorded by Karen Lafferty
on *Sweet Communion*, © Capitol Christian Music Group

By the time I graduated with my Bachelor of Music Education, I needed a break. I was still thinking of pursuing a master's degree and making a career in music education. But I decided to give entertainment a try instead and see if I got any breaks. If nothing came of it, I figured teaching would always be a safe backup.

I headed back to the Ruidoso area and hired on as a solo entertainer at a small steak house called the Inncredible. I performed four to five hours a night behind the inn's horseshoe-shaped bar. Once I sat down, customers could only see my upper body and guitar. They had no idea I had a kick drum and high hat cymbals under the bar. Once I started playing, and they heard the percussion, they were amazed. I loved the steak house staff and atmosphere, and I worked hard to expand my repertoire, learning a long list of country and pop songs.

While working at the Inncredible that summer, I met a vacationing couple who owned hotels in Scottsdale, Arizona, and New Orleans, Louisiana. They invited me to work in their clubs, starting in Scottsdale. I was excited! Working for these people would allow me to travel to major cities as an entertainer, fulfilling one of my goals.

I worked first in Scottsdale at an expensive restaurant, roving and singing from table to table, entertaining the snowbirds. The New Orleans hotel was under construction and was behind schedule for completion, so my friends connected me with a job at a restaurant called Caruso's in Fort Worth, Texas. Working there turned out to be an unexpected challenge. Caruso's was a dark, dingy place, even in the daylight, and rumored to have Mafia-type connections. I was so naive going in that I was wide open to being compromised and manipulated.

The owner, Mr. Caruso, was a fat older man who treated the women who worked for him like personal call girls. He flirted with me, trying to entice me. "I'm glad you've come to work with me. You'll like it here." I was uncomfortable with his "remember who the boss here is" personality. I determined to avoid him as much as possible and stay focused on the music.

One night, Caruso began chatting casually with me about the local music scene in Dallas. I was eager to experience the nightlife in the big city. When he invited me to listen to live music at some other clubs, I jumped at the opportunity.

It's hard to imagine now that I could have been so dumb at age twenty-two as to think I could control that crafty old man. That night, as we drove, Caruso pulled the car over in a dark residential area and shut off the engine.

"Why, are you stopping?" I asked, my heart pounding. The possibility of rape flashed through my mind. He reached over and pulled me across the bench seat toward him.

"C'mon, let's get close," he cooed.

He frightened me. "I'm not interested in that kind of relationship with you, Mr. Caruso!" My heart stopped as he suddenly grabbed my hand and jammed it down into his pants.

I was stunned—and afraid of this powerful man. For a split second, I thought I had to do what he expected. It made me sick.

No! I don't have to do this! Jerking my hand back, I jumped out of the car and fled into the darkness. Caruso followed me. I was fortunate, or more than likely, God graciously intervened at that point.

"Look," he said, pulling alongside me. "I'm sorry."

"This isn't what I came here for!" I sputtered. "I am *not* one of your girls, so don't even think about it!"

"All right, I get it, just let me take you home," he said.

"And you keep your hands off of me!"

"Sure, sure," he agreed.

Thankfully, Caruso took me straight home. Too many young girls thought they had to do his bidding. I couldn't. The next day, I quit the club and arranged to move in with some of my former sorority sisters working in Dallas.

I'd just had one of the most frightening encounters of my life with a man, yet I also had one of the best during the brief time I lived in Fort Worth. While I was in Ruidoso, I had met a guy named Steve. He was a pilot and an up-and-coming Dallas businessman. We began seriously dating when I moved to Texas.

I had never been treated so well by a man before. I could find no fault in him, which challenged my cynical belief that all men were users and liars. His tender care gave me hope that this could be the loving and healthy relationship I had craved for so long.

In the following months, I let my guard down to become intimate with him. *What did it matter?* I thought, trying to quell the pang of guilt. After all, we were hinting around about marriage. Steve had no religious background. He said he was "open-minded" about God and that if we had kids, he wouldn't mind if I took them to church.

Steve and I continued seeing each other as much as our schedules and travels allowed. When the hotel in New Orleans was finally ready in late February of 1971, I got on my way to Louisiana. I felt secure thinking that Steve wanted to be part of my new adventure.

New Orleans is a magical city full of Dixieland music and good times. I fully intended to embrace the musical experience and the fun it had to offer. And I thought, *No one knows me here. I can do what I want, and nobody will know.*

But God knew. He strategically located the Roadway Inn where I worked right across the street from a Baptist church. Knowing it was "the right thing to do" in my heart, I started going to church there. Some folks in the congregation raised their eyebrows when they heard I was playing in a bar, but others were friendlier and prayed for me. A couple of people even came to the bar to listen to me.

I'd been a wholesome, teetotaling Baptist girl when I went off to college, but working as a barroom entertainer turned me increasingly toward loose living. I still believed God was real, and I still had a fuzzy conviction about somehow being an encouragement and witness through my music. But my moral compromise deepened in New Orleans. I would drink too much, get sick, feel guilty, make bad decisions—and then wonder why I had done it.

My relationship with Steve suffered, as one thing after another kept him from coming to New Orleans to visit me. His car broke down, and he broke a leg. Then an old college boyfriend, who was now a New York entertainer, came to New Orleans. We dated and made the Out on the Town page of the New Orleans newspaper. I felt like a jerk for sneaking around on Steve, but I got caught up in the excitement of my new adventures. The longer Steve and I were apart, the more unsure I became of my feelings for him and our future together. I began seeing other guys.

I found myself increasingly playing a game designed to get the attention I desired, singing raunchy songs and making crude remarks for the laughs they got me. I got angry with myself whenever I slipped up and drank too much. My head ached from my hangovers, but my spirit was hurting too.

The thing I struggled most to escape was insecurity. I performed so people would like and appreciate me, and I had the crazy idea that they wouldn't notice me if I didn't have my guitar.

Who was I? What did I have to offer the broken people in these places? I had started out wanting to do something good with my music. Instead, I was using it to make me feel like I had a purpose. I compromised my morals to stand out, dousing the little bit of light I tried to shine. I had become a chameleon, acting out one role in the bars and another at home and church. I was a hypocrite, playing games and messing with fire.

My biggest and final fling in New Orleans was Mardi Gras, a celebration filled with parades, parties, and drunkenness. My friends and I jumped right into the Mardi Gras party spirit. I wasn't into hard drug use, but I partied hard on alcohol. My soul was conflicted between wanting to do the right things and not having the power to do so.

Through it all, God kept his hand on me. I continued attending the Baptist church, hoping to climb out of the pit I was digging for myself. I felt so dirty and like such a failure in my faith. Then, amid my struggle, a light came on, the kind that signals change: *If I* truly *believe that God wants me to live for him*, I asked myself, *why do I do these things?*

One evening, a guy spoke at the church about a Christian coffeehouse he ran in the French Quarter called the Way. This guy was getting out there with the people, the "publicans and sinners." Some folks at the Baptist church told me that the only way to witness for Christ was through the way we lived—an apparent condemnation of my lifestyle. But this guy and the coffeehouse were taking the gospel right to the people, sharing Jesus most naturally. The idea of it stirred something deep within me. I thought, *If Jesus were here, that's what he'd be doing.* In response, I wrote my first Christian song, "The Way."

Then Rhonda arrived.

Rhonda Ray was a mellow, fun hometown girl who had been one of my best friends in high school. Short and dark-haired, she was also part of the group of girls I ran around with from the Baptist church in Alamogordo. After high school, Rhonda had gone to New Mexico State University in Las Cruces and gotten involved with Campus Crusade for Christ. It was clear that her understanding of God and her daily walk with him had grown deeper since our school days.

We'd kept in touch through letters and visits. During my time in New Orleans, she sent me a small Campus Crusade booklet titled "Have You Made the Wonderful Discovery of the Spirit-Filled Life?" Part of me wanted to tell her to quit preaching. Another part of me was curious to know how and why her experience was so different from mine. When Rhonda came to visit me in New Orleans, the Lord used her to open my eyes to what it was like to lead a Spirit-filled life.

She came spouting things like "Praise the Lord!" about everything from sunsets to parking spaces "miraculously" opening up. I had never heard people praise the Lord at all in this manner, much less out loud and in public. She would say, "Let's pray before shopping," another new concept for me. She believed God would help us find deals and that he wanted to be involved in those kinds of everyday things. Rhonda also had no problem coming to the Roadway

Inn lounge to listen to me. She would sit in the bar and talk to people about her faith without condemnation. Her life radiated Jesus.

I felt a little guilty around Rhonda, but I was hungry for the kind of life she had more than anything. When I finally considered what was in the booklet she'd sent, the first thing that hit me was that I, not God, was at the center of my life. Although I was a believer, I was only a "carnal Christian" (1 Corinthians 3:1–3 KJV) at best. *My* self, *my* desires, and *my* wishes superseded God's. Next, I saw that I depended on my human strength to overcome my weaknesses instead of the Holy Spirit's power.

No wonder I hadn't been able to conquer the sin and confusion in my life! I needed to live like I genuinely believed in God, let Jesus be Lord, and live by the power of the Spirit. I had a sudden revelation of God's love for me, of his grace and undeserved favor. I wanted to change, not out of duty but out of sheer love.

I began to see and believe that God had a plan for my life for the first time. I prayed. I didn't just want to wear the name "Christian," I wanted to be a genuine follower of Jesus wherever I was. I was tired of playing games and being a hypocrite—I wanted to become the person God intended me to be.

After Rhonda left, I started reading the Bible daily, and it came alive to me! Even my thinking about what my work in the bar should look like underwent a life-changing shift. I began receiving the guidance I so desperately needed through the Word of God. I had taken a big step forward. Campus Crusade was about to become the next important milestone in my life. It would help me discover what it meant to walk daily with Christ, teaching me how to share my faith and launching me in a new direction.

CHAPTER 6

Salt and Light

Father, where am I going?
Father, I'll rest in knowing
That you love me,
And you will guide me along.

—"Father of Lights" by Karen Lafferty, from *Sweet Communion*
© Capitol Christian Music Group

When Rhonda visited me, she told me about Music Week, an upcoming event in Arrowhead Springs, California, hosted by Campus Crusade for Christ. She said it was geared toward training musicians to reach people for Christ through music and intentionally sharing their faith. It sounded like just what I needed, so with my new relationship with the Lord and a newfound vision, I packed up my car and headed for California.

The teaching at the camp blew me away. I learned so much from speakers like Josh McDowell, who taught on apologetics—the defense of Christianity. They led us deeper into worship with songs like "Pass It On" and "He's Everything to Me." And they taught us how to communicate our faith in Christ boldly.

Our instruction about evangelism included getting on a bus for Newport Beach. There, two by two, we went out to meet and talk to people about Jesus. My partner and I spotted a woman with a little girl at the beach and sat down to chat with them. It was my turn to speak while my partner prayed.

I explained why we were there and asked her, "Would you be willing to go through this booklet with me?" When she said yes, I fumbled through a pamphlet titled "The Four Spiritual Laws," stumbling over the words. *It's all good practice*, I thought, *but I sure messed that up!* When we got to the prayer at the end, God showed me the power of his gospel.

I explained how she could give her life to the Lord, and I asked, "Would you like to receive the Lord?"

"Yes, I would," she replied. I was shocked—and encouraged! My faith and boldness took a giant leap forward that day.

I was surprised to discover that I was not the first person to write a contemporary Christian song. I met numerous people who were writing songs about having a relationship with Jesus. Seeing Christian musicians share their faith through music convinced me that this was what I wanted to do with my life. I auditioned to join the Campus Crusade music ministry and participate in one of their bands, which would involve ongoing training and discipleship. Since I had more musical training and experience in performance than most of those who also auditioned, I thought it was a given that they would want me.

Then the directors began asking me questions. "If you were accepted and there wasn't room on the music staff, would you be willing to serve in another area of ministry?"

I said, "No, not really. My focus and calling is music, and I have music training. That's where I should work."

They scribbled something in their notes, probably to the effect that I was not willing to serve, and then they asked me if I would be able to join right away and go through staff training.

"No, I have to go back to the steak house in Ruidoso and work at least one more summer because I have changed so much that I want to share with my friends. Oh, and I am going to compete soon in the Miss New Mexico Pageant, so I have to finish that as well."

They wrote it all down in their notes, perhaps making special mention about working in a bar and steak house. After the audition, there were eighteen finalists selected, and I wasn't one of them. I was stunned and a bit humiliated. *What's the matter with these people? Don't they know I'm called to music ministry?* The rejection was hard to take, but God had just asked me to do things his way, not mine.

I immediately went to my small group leaders.

"I know I'm supposed to do this!" I said.

"You said you've given your life to the Lord and trusted your future to him—trust that he will open up some other doors for you," they told me. "When God closes one door, he opens another. Pray and look for his timing."

I couldn't see it at the time, but their counsel turned out to be sound. As I learned to trust him, God guided me forward. I went back to New Mexico thinking I was only supposed to be "salt and light" in the entertainment world. But God began doing a purifying work in my heart, helping me be faithful to him no matter where I was. There was no more playing the entertainment game, dishonoring the Lord in my music, or putting on a spiritual facade while loving sin in the secret places of my heart. I offered my failures to him in exchange for a fresh start and a new purpose. I asked the Holy Spirit to help me resist temptation, and with his aid, I began trusting God to guide my choices rather than merely reacting to things that came my way.

I returned to Ruidoso and spent the summer sharing my faith with old friends. I saw my audiences in a whole new light. These were people with needs and heartbreaks just like mine— people in need of the same redemptive revelation.

The Lord showed me three areas I needed to change to honor him and have integrity as an entertainer. First, I was accountable for every word that came out of my mouth (Proverbs 18:21; Ephesians 4:29), which meant I had to drop the songs from my repertoire that encouraged immorality. There were still plenty of good songs to sing. Second, I needed to stop drinking if I wanted people to see my life as complete in Jesus. It wasn't that drinking itself was wrong. He wanted me to draw strength through the Holy Spirit (Ephesians 5:18) rather than settle for the false courage that comes from alcohol. Third, I was to try to love people as Jesus did. I knew I could accomplish all three things with God's Holy Spirit to empower me.

I still sang some of the hit songs my customers requested, and God showed me ways to use them as a witness. Before singing "Help Me Make It through the Night," I'd invite the audience to listen to what that poor woman was going through. When the song concluded, I'd say, "If I had a chance to talk to that woman, I'd sing. . . ," and then I'd begin "Put Your Hand in the Hand." In other songs, I'd change a few words. Instead of singing "Then you and I would simply fly away" at the end of Bread's song, "If," I sang "You and I would simply fly away, away with my Jesus." The lyrics to many pop songs were either Christian or could be rendered in a Christian context, implying that Jesus was the one who made the difference. As I looked for ways to reinterpret lyrics, it became easier to witness during a nightclub act.

My new approach to entertainment at the Inncredible was not the only reflection of my changed heart and values. I headed to Hobbs to compete in the Miss New Mexico Pageant later that summer. I saw the competition less as a possibility to entertain people and launch my career and more as an opportunity to focus on others. As we moved through the different phases of the pageant, I genuinely tried to be a friend to the other girls, who were under a lot of stress with the competition. I earned first runner-up in the pageant. And I was named Miss Congeniality—a humbling surprise and testimony to what God will do when we care for others the way he does.

That summer, I heard the Holy Spirit was moving in a church in El Paso, Texas. Since I believed the Spirit was also moving in me, I visited the Jesus Chapel to see what was happening. As the congregation worshiped, hands began going up all over the room, raised in praise and worship—something I'd never seen or done before. It made me nervous, but something inside of me wanted to join them anyway. We started singing "Thy Loving Kindness," and I closed my eyes and raised my hands when we sang, "I will lift up my hands unto your name." As I did, I felt a new freedom in worship!

After that summer in Ruidoso, I had a new confidence that I could be Christ's witness in the entertainment industry. I still hoped that I could someday join Campus Crusade and be involved in their music ministry. But at that point, I chose to continue working as an entertainer. New Mexico wasn't a place where a performer could do big things. I considered my options. New York was too far away and scary for this New Mexico girl; Nashville was too country; California seemed right. I also had relatives there, which would make the leap safer and easier. I had no idea God was using *my* plan to get me where he wanted me to be in *his* plan.

If I were going to make a splash—and a living—in California, I knew I had to find ways to sell my talent before heading out. I got a book about the music business, including contact information for agents and studios. I put together a publicity packet, complete with photos, a personally written bio, and homemade business cards I'd stamped out by hand. A friend at the local radio station helped me cut a demo of three or four songs. I sent out fifty packets to studios, agents, and managers in the Hollywood area. I received twelve responses: six contacts declined me, and six invited me for interviews.

After I finished my stint at the Inncredible, I packed up my Volkswagen Squareback. I hit the road, praying to God that if there were any Christians in California he would lead me to them. I wasn't even sure if my Uncle Marley, Aunt Betty, and cousins were believers. All I knew about California was what I had heard: there were hippies and weird people in abundance.

Traveling on Interstate 10, I passed Palm Springs and began to see the infamous, low-lying bank of brown Los Angeles smog.

It made me nervous. *Yikes! How is a country bumpkin like me going to make it in a place like this?*

I found my way to my aunt and uncle's house in Costa Mesa on a Saturday. Once I got there, I asked my cousin Rock if he and his wife Ana went to church anywhere. They got excited and said, "Oh yes! We both got saved at Calvary Chapel—go with us tomorrow!"

As soon as we stepped onto the grounds of Calvary Chapel, I sensed a life-giving atmosphere. It was a delightful, come-as-you-are fellowship where I was greeted with smiles and hugs from young hippies who had become Jesus freaks. I particularly remember a sandy-haired guy named Tommy Coomes, who had a "fro" and a beard that reached his chest. Later, I found out he was part of Love Song, one of the first "Jesus music" bands to come out of Calvary Chapel.

The whole place vibrated with joyful praise! Many songs that morning were familiar hymns, but this congregation sang the old songs as if they were the day's contemporary hits. I had once complained about hymns being old-fashioned and irrelevant. Now we were worshiping with those songs as the believers who first wrote them must have done.

When Pastor Chuck Smith announced the scriptural text for his sermon, Bibles appeared everywhere. What a scene! All those people, young and old, digging into the Word of God together—so rich and alive!

Pastor Chuck concluded with an invitation to anyone who had not yet given their life to the Lord. Several responded, and we applauded them as they made their way down the crowded aisles to the front, where they prayed to receive Christ. Ushers then pointed them to a side room for instruction about growing as new followers of Jesus.

We concluded the service by standing and singing, "Love, love, love, love; Christians, this is your call." As I swayed to the music, my arms around those on either side of me, I marveled at long-haired hippies with their arms around short-haired Christians in business suits next to them. *Wow, God! Where have you brought me? I didn't think I would see this until heaven!*

I didn't know it yet, but I had landed in the heart of the Jesus movement that was sweeping the nation and radically changing the lives of thousands of young people. I was about to be carried into the current of what God was doing. Once there, he would set the stage for the lifelong ministry he intended for me.

I soon began taking steps toward breaking into the LA music entertainment business. My first interview was with the lawyer who managed folksinger Joan Baez. He got out my packet, saying he had listened to the demo.

"What did you do before you came here?" he asked.

"I finished my music degree at Eastern New Mexico University with the idea of becoming a choir director. But what I want now is to be an entertainer," I replied. I had just answered like the wet-behind-the-ears rookie I was, not a professional with performance experience under her belt. After three minutes, he dismissed me, saying I should return to New Mexico and be a music teacher. I left his office deflated.

The funniest interview I had was on the Sunset Strip in West Hollywood. I parked, went into the elegant black high-rise, and took the elevator several floors up when I arrived. When I found the office, I noticed a sign that said Motown Records. Sure enough, I was standing at the door of the home of soul music USA!

"My name is Karen Lafferty," I timidly told the receptionist. "I have an appointment with Lindy Blaskey."

"Oh yes," she said, "he's waiting for you, right this way." As we walked, I passed a man who was wearing sunglasses and a flat cap. I didn't discover until later that I had just come within arm's length of Stevie Wonder!

I seated myself in front of thin, handsome Lindy Blaskey, still surprised to be in his high-rise office. He was every bit the publishing professional, yet always very personable.

"I'm not Motown material. So what am I doing here?" I asked.

He laughed. "I'm leaving Motown to help start a new record company, and we're looking for new artists and songwriters."

"Have you listened to my demo?"

"Yes. I heard your music a couple of years ago."

"What! How is that possible?"

"A woman agent I know heard you at a Bob Hope event in New Mexico. She circulated the demo you gave her to some record companies here."

I was amazed to hear that he already had a file on me.

"I like your songs," he said. "If we can get them placed with a known artist, I'd like to offer you a publishing deal with two of your songs."

That blew me away! "By the way, what's the name of the new company?" I asked.

"It's one of Hugh Hefner's companies," he explained, "called Playboy Records." By then, Blaskey knew I was a Christian and noticed I was a bit taken aback. He hadn't been impressed with my outgoing Christianity. When he found out I lived in Orange County, he said, "Isn't that where Jesus left his sandals?" But Blaskey assured me that the new record company had nothing to do with the Playboy Club or Playboy Magazine—it was merely a record company. After that, he always referred to me as "Pat Boone's girl," though I had never met Boone.

I agreed to the deal reluctantly because I still wasn't sure I wanted to associate myself with Playboy. Blaskey arranged for me to record two of my songs in a well-appointed Hollywood studio. I got a taste of professional recording, complete with professional Hollywood studio musicians. They cut my selections on a 45 rpm demo. When they finished, Blaskey pitched it to see if other artists might be interested in recording one or both songs. No one picked them up, but I still have the demo with the Playboy Records label on it.

My best interview of all was with Ken Kragen. He managed stars such as Kenny Rogers, the New Christy Minstrels, Lionel Richie, Olivia Newton-John, and the Bee Gees. He asked questions about my music and goals before informing me they weren't taking on any new artists at that time. He also offered me some sound advice.

"Get a job around here," he said. "You have some potential, but you need to work somewhere where people can hear you and get to know you, where you can gain more experience and make contacts. Managers and agents want to see what you do in front of people, not just hear your little demo. Also, try to get yourself booked at a showcase club like the Ice House or the Troubadour."

I followed his advice and played at the Ice House showcase in Pasadena one night. I also found work entertaining in restaurants in Orange County. Working in Los Angeles would have been better in a professional sense. But it became evident later that God was directing me, even in that.

Some had told me it would be hard to find good entertainment jobs, but I found that it wasn't hard at all if I was pleasant and dependable. Also, the restaurant jobs paid well and provided a much healthier working atmosphere than bars and clubs. I landed jobs at the Plankhouse in Huntington Beach and the Moonraker in Santa Ana. They were the best and most comfortable entertainment jobs I had ever had.

I earned a whopping $500 a week—big money back then. With a steady income coming in, I moved into a small apartment. Since I was still in Orange County, I continued attending Calvary Chapel and went as often as possible. It seemed to me I was finally on the road to bigger and better things.

CHAPTER 7

Called

I'm going to trust your Spirit
To speak to the hearts who will hear it.
And I'm going out to share it in my life.
Lord, can you hear?
My life is yours; my life is yours,
Jesus, my life is yours.

—"My Life Is Yours" by Karen Lafferty, from *Life Pages—Love of the Ages*
© Capitol Christian Music Group

Calvary Chapel had been a conservative church until the local hippie population encountered Jesus. Pastor Chuck was concerned for the many young people caught up in the whirlwind forces of the '60s—rock music, drugs, free love, and Eastern religion. When the door opened for him to reach out to them, he did so with a passion that changed the entire church.

I heard that church leaders had put up a sign saying, "Shoes Required to Enter." They had just installed new carpeting in the sanctuary, and some were afraid the hippies would wreck it with their dirty, oily bare feet. Chuck's response was: "If the carpet is more important to you than accommodating the young people God is sending to us, I will have it ripped up." The carpet stayed, the sign came down, and the hippies kept coming.

Pastor Chuck got connected with a young evangelist named Lonnie Frisbee through his teenage kids. Frisbee looked like a modern-day John the Baptist, and he was leading hippies and surfers to the Lord in droves. After baptizing new believers in the ocean, he took them to Calvary Chapel for discipleship. They felt at home in this come-as-you-are setting, sitting on the floor as close as they could get to where Pastor Chuck was teaching.

Calvary Chapel became my second home. I attended Bible studies whenever I wasn't entertaining somewhere. They instilled in me an abiding love for God's Word. All around me, young believers like me were thriving in this hothouse of spiritual growth and reaching out to our generation through their music and testimonies. I wanted to be part of it all!

Music was one way I knew I could be involved. I asked if I could share one of my songs sometime. At that point, Calvary's Sunday morning services were still quite traditional, with hymns accompanied by organ and piano. They directed me to Tom Stipe, a softhearted associate pastor sporting a headful of big, bushy hair. He was also a musician, record producer, and Bible teacher. Tom asked me questions about my relationship with the Lord, and I sang one of my songs for him. Afterward, he told me about their Monday morning musicians' fellowship. He also mentioned that Monday night was youth night, and musicians could play their songs there.

Once I was given the okay to join the fellowship and shared my songs at the Monday night youth service, they added me to the list of on-call musicians. Those whose names were on the list could be invited at any time to play at diverse venues.

Calvary Chapel was becoming known for having a pool of gifted musicians willing to minister whenever invited. For us, no invitation was too small or unimportant to accept as an opportunity to shine our light for Jesus. It was excellent training in humility and readiness to minister to a wide range of audiences.

I often performed at convalescent homes and grew to love my elderly audiences. I pulled out familiar hymns and popular songs from their generation so they could enjoy and participate in the music. Organizers called on me to perform on the Tomorrowland stage at Disneyland and at the Good Time Saloon at Knott's Berry Farm. The "list" kept me busy. The only downside was having to say no to an invitation to a coffeehouse or youth group because I was still working nights as a restaurant entertainer at the time.

In the Maranatha! musicians' fellowship, it seemed we all came with some "baggage" from our before-Christ years. Some were awaiting court dates for past drug use. Many had broken relationships. We didn't have it all together, but we all were seeking to change. There were no wagging fingers and "you must change first" attitudes. Once you were part of the fellowship, you were considered available to testify about what the Lord had done in your life.

Although the praise music for which we would become known was already starting to spring up in our fellowship, our first songs were testimonial in nature. Our primary goal was to bring people to the Lord. During this time, the rapid growth of Calvary Chapel called for a more spacious place to meet. They purchased land a block away from the original church, setting up a giant circus tent while constructing a sanctuary. Busloads of people would arrive from other churches, mingling with young seekers who came in off the streets. We presented evangelistic concerts under the tent every Saturday night (which continued for thirteen years). Usually, a soloist like me would begin, followed by a band. Then one of our young evangelists, such as Greg Laurie, Tom Stipe, or Jimmy Kempner, gave a short gospel message. I was often moved to tears as hundreds of people came forward to receive Christ.

One spring break, around a hundred of us decided to go to Lake Havasu near the Colorado River and set up stages by London Bridge to do some concerts. We camped out during the week we were there and had open worship times around the campfire that rang throughout the campground. Mean-spirited members of a biker gang made fun of us, and we even had a streaker in camp one night. But in the end, some of them came to the Lord.

We were a group of Jesus people carrying giant Bibles and bundles of tracts, going places, playing our music, and sharing about the Lord. We were always looking for opportunities to do concerts in public places so that non-Christians could hear the gospel. Wherever crowds gathered, we played and testified. It was all about getting our generation to come to Jesus.

I clearly remember the night in 1972 when I felt a distinct call into ministry. I had just finished entertaining at the Plankhouse. I was sitting at the bar, having a Coke, and talking with the bartender and some customers. One guy began mocking me and ridiculing goody-two-shoes Christians. He was one of the regulars, a man who had attempted suicide a couple of months before. It was an intense conversation. As I tried to share the Lord with him, he cut me off and said, "I can't believe you believe that. That is so stupid!" I left in tears because he was so lost.

I went home from the Plankhouse that evening thinking about the kinds of songs I sang every night—"Mr. Bojangles," "Raindrops Keep Falling on My Head," "La Bamba." My music repertoire—including Christian songs—didn't seem to be impacting anyone's life. The songs were entertaining and relaxing, which wasn't bad, but I knew how much people were hurting and needed answers in life. I *knew* the Answer—what was I doing to lead them to him?

I thought of Matthew 9:36: "When he (Jesus) saw the crowds, he had compassion on them because they were confused and helpless, like sheep without a shepherd" (NLT). I realized then that it was not enough to salt my song list with a few Christian tunes. I needed to move once and for all from mere entertainment to playing music for a greater purpose—to make a difference. I needed to sing *the truth*.

That night, I said yes to the call of God, setting the course for the rest of my life.

After only four months working at the restaurants, I went to my boss and gave my two weeks' notice.

"What? Aren't we paying you enough?" he asked.

"No, it's a great job," I said.

"Why, then?" he asked. "Somebody offer you a better job?"

"Well, yes," I replied. "The Lord."

"Oh no," he groaned. "You're doing that Christian thing." But he had studied to be a priest at one time, so he understood what I was doing to some degree.

I called my mom, thinking she'd be excited because she'd been the one who led me to the Lord and championed my music.

"Mom!" I blurted out. "I quit my job, and I'm going into *ministry*!"

"Oh, so you'll be on salary with the church now?" she asked.

"No, Mom. They call it living by faith. I'll get some offerings when I sing, and I'll teach guitar lessons on the side."

"But why would you leave your paying job? You've been able to witness to people there, and you said you led one fellow to the Lord." There was a momentary silence at the other end of the line. "You do remember I'm the cosigner on your car loan. If you can't make the payments, I'll have to," she said sternly.

"Mom, where the Lord guides, the Lord will provide," I assured her.

"I don't understand. But if you feel that way, I guess you must do it."

I was disappointed that she wasn't excited about me going into ministry. I knew then I couldn't write home for money; I was on my own.

What had I just done?

God had called me out of the best-paying and most secure job I'd ever had, while at the same time changing the goals I had been striving to achieve as I sought to be a light in the entertainment world. I stepped out only knowing that this was what I was supposed to do, at a time when there were few Christian musicians in ministry to use as role models.

One thing was clear: I was in new territory. It was going to be God or nothing from then on.

CHAPTER 8

Seek Ye First

"Seek ye first the kingdom of God, and his righteousness;
and all these things shall be added unto you."

—Matthew 6:33 (KJV)

The seeming rejection I had experienced while seeking a Campus Crusade music position had taught me that when God closes one door, he opens another. My recent call to ministry gave me opportunities to expand my perspective and trust God in new ways.

Pastor Chuck (we affectionately called him Papa Chuck) warned us about the realities of serving in full-time ministry. At a retreat, he asked us: "Do you really want to be in ministry?" He probed our hearts, asking questions and sharing with us his difficulties and disappointments.

"It can look exciting, but get ready for hard things," he said. "If you want to do it despite the difficulties, you're probably called. But if I can talk you out of it, you're probably not called. If God puts passion in your heart for ministry, it will keep you going for years."

He was right. The day I left the Plankhouse, I stepped out of what the world calls "normal" and "responsible" and faced my first hurdle—finances. It was the first big test of my resolve in the face of doubts and challenging circumstances.

I no longer had a regular job, but the rent and bills still came due without fail. I shopped thrift stores and managed to outfit my tiny apartment in Santa Ana with a mattress, a card table, and two chairs, which I painted orange. Boards and bricks made a workable bookcase, and I found an inflatable couch, probably designed for a swimming pool. I had no television, but not having one suited me just fine since I spent so much time writing songs. To my little dog Snow and me, it felt like home.

I started teaching guitar, seeking students through the church. However, at $5.00 an hour, my income didn't nearly cover the bills. I lived frugally, existing mainly on peanut butter and jelly sandwiches. I was genuinely grateful whenever someone invited me out for a meal.

When my savings ran out and the rent came due, I panicked. I thought, *Maybe I'm out of the Lord's will. Maybe I shouldn't have quit my job. Did I hear from God?* I had a hard choice to make. I could swallow my pride and disappointment and go back to work in the bars, or I could choose to trust God and keep going.

Thankfully, I was part of a fellowship of believers who taught and believed the Word. That night I attended a Bible study led by Ken Gulliksen. He was teaching from the Sermon on the Mount, in which Jesus tells us not to worry about what we will eat, drink, or wear. Jesus says the Father feeds the birds of the air and clothes the lilies of the field and that we are more valuable than they. He says: "Seek ye first the kingdom of God, and his righteousness; and all these things shall be added unto you" (Matthew 6:33 KJV). Those words burned in my heart! There was my answer—my job was to seek God above all else and take him at his word, and his job was to honor his promise.

The rent was still not paid when I returned home that night, but my joy and faith had returned. I had peace in my heart that God was going to take care of me. I didn't know *how* he would do it but knowing that he *promised* to do it renewed my faith.

Thinking about these truths, I picked up my guitar. A lot of the praise songs we were composing at that time were Scripture set to music. I knew these verses from Matthew were important, so I began writing. First, I created a simple melody on my guitar and then set God's words to the music:

> Seek ye first the kingdom of God,
> And his righteousness;
> And all these things shall be added unto you.

I needed something to finish the phrase, so I tacked on a couple of alleluias, thinking that would make it easier for people to remember:

> Seek ye first the kingdom of God,
> And his righteousness;
> And all these things shall be added unto you.
> Allelu, Alleluia.

I played the song several times, enjoying how the Scriptures came to life through the melody. Then I developed a simple descant to be sung over the original tune, making the song more memorable and causing it to burst with the joy of its simple truth. I titled the piece "Seek Ye First" and recorded the final version on my cassette recorder. I was excited to sing it at the Monday night Bible study.

I had already started sharing some of my songs at the Monday night gathering. When I approached Pastor Chuck and said, "I have a new song God gave me. Could I sing it tonight?" he gave me the go-ahead. When I taught "Seek Ye First" to those gathered at Calvary Chapel that evening, everyone learned it quickly. Pastor Chuck said to me, "That is beautiful," which meant a lot to me, coming from him.

As "Seek Ye First" took its place in our regular worship, we discovered other Scripture verses that fit the song's simple melody and message. Two verses, in particular, seemed appropriate to add—Matthew 4:4 and 7:7—because they reminded us that God was everything we needed:

Man shall not live by bread alone,
But by every word
That proceeds from the mouth of God.
Allelu, Alleluia

Ask, and it shall be given unto you;
Seek, and ye shall find;
Knock, and the door shall be opened unto you.
Allelu, Alleluia

During that time, I still sensed a strong pull toward Campus Crusade's ministry and thought God was calling me to do their month-long training program. But the tuition was $400, and I still needed money for food and rent.

Earlier, I had contacted the Miss New Mexico Pageant board to see if I could use the $750 education scholarship I had won for Bible training. Then I waited. A few days after writing "Seek Ye First," I received a call from the pageant board telling me that they were authorizing me to use the money for Bible training for the first time. Furthermore, I could use any money left over for whatever I wanted. That check covered the tuition and also my rent, car payment, gas, and food. God was "adding these things" to me—beyond my expectations!

I drove to Arrowhead Springs to participate in Campus Crusade's training program at the Institute of Biblical Studies. It was terrific, and I loved it. However, I found I no longer felt led to join their staff at the end of the course. It was clear that I needed to go back to Calvary Chapel to see what God had in store for me.

I began to learn what it meant to be a full-time Christian musician. I made my way with the Lord's help, applying the diligence I had learned from my mom by working hard, seizing opportunities, and being frugal. I continued teaching guitar and singing in a few places for offerings. Maranatha! Music paid me for playing and singing on recordings and for writing out lead sheets. All these things added up so that I could eat and pay my rent while growing in ministry.

God's answer to my asking, seeking, knocking was a whole lot bigger than just paying the rent and living expenses, however.

He would soon take my simple, singable little song and use it to open doors, sending me down a path with exciting kingdom purposes I couldn't have dreamed up on my own. But along with the joy, just as Pastor Chuck had said, there would be tough lessons and disappointments ahead. Thankfully, I had already learned a foundational lesson I would need along the way: Don't shake your fist at God and run away from him amid troubles. Instead, take him at his word and run *to* him.

CHAPTER 9

Jesus Musicians

Why should the devil have all the good music?

—"Why Should the Devil Have All the Good Music?" by Larry Norman
from *Only Visiting This Planet*, ©1972 Verve Records

As the Jesus movement grew, Calvary Chapel continued to be a spiritual growth and music ministry hotbed. My musician friends and I were doing what we loved for the One we loved, thanks to the careful, prayerful guidance of some wonderful spiritual fathers. We didn't realize at the time that we were helping launch a powerful new wave of Christian music.

Our church leaders were very intentional in discipling us to do our music ministry in the right way. Two things sum up what God wanted from us—a right heart and a humble attitude. The ministry to which so many of us felt called needed to be walked out in truth if we wanted to reach people.

As our fellowship and the demand for our musicians grew, so did the need for organization and management. Out of practical necessity, Pastor Chuck had created Maranatha! Music in 1971 as a resource for the growing number of "Jesus musicians." He'd envisioned a company that would not only meet our need for more hands-on guidance but which could also provide financial support. That support would come by way of individual recording projects for those involved in the music ministry. Pastor Chuck himself put up the money for Maranatha! Music's first collaborative album. *The Everlastin' Living Jesus Music Concert* album consisted of testimonial and worship songs from Calvary Chapel musicians.

The concept of worship bands—or Christian music artists in general—was relatively unheard of when Maranatha! Music was developing. We chose to call ourselves Jesus musicians. We wrestled with what to call our new kind of music, how to keep it untainted by pride, and whether it was okay to feature individual musicians performing solos. When artists did solos, they were careful to give God the glory. We sought to be humble and natural in how we dressed and presented ourselves, striving to promote Jesus above all else.

Pastor Chuck and other church leaders encouraged honesty and humility in our relationships and service, using God's Word to address situations that came up. Once, during a Monday morning Maranatha! musicians' fellowship, a guitar player named Dave got up to share.

"Hey, everybody," he began, "I need to ask you all for forgiveness for something. A lot of you know I was part of the band at the concert Saturday night. Pastor Romaine approached me after the concert and said, 'Dave, I've watched you play a lot and have always felt like you were playing for the Lord. But tonight, as I watched you, it seemed you were playing to impress the girls in the front row.' Know what? He was right. God totally busted me. Please forgive me for playing my music for myself and not for Jesus."

Pastor Chuck came with a letter in hand and a look of concern on his face on another occasion. The letter was from a pastor who had hosted one of our groups. The band had played a rock evangelism concert for youth and then played the same set in the Sunday morning service where the older audience was unprepared for that style of music. The pastor wrote: *If your musicians can't be more sensitive to who is in the audience; if they don't understand ministry any better than that, we don't want your groups anymore.*

With fatherly sternness, Pastor Chuck said, "I don't ever want to get a letter like this again." He was disappointed that some of us had not yet learned that ministry was about presenting Jesus to people in a way they could understand and not about being cool. That sat heavily on my heart. It was a lesson I never forgot.

Over the years, I came up with my own way of explaining what Pastor Chuck was teaching us through the Word and by example about how to do music ministry in a church. First and foremost, we musicians had to have a *right heart*, offering our music first to God in faith and pleasing him. Then we had to show sensitivity and respect toward our audiences. But it worked in both directions. We also needed to help our audiences understand that it was not about style but *our hearts*. Love Song, one of our early bands, wrote "Little Country Church" to help churches see past outward things like the length of our hair, what we wore, or the type of music we played.

During this time, God engineered an event that further expanded my thinking about music ministry. I was still teaching guitar lessons to help pay bills, and the church had given me a phone number for a fellow named Jimmy Owens. I assumed he was a kid looking for guitar lessons. Since I was heading to the beach that day with friends, I took the number with me. Later that afternoon, I called from an open payphone and introduced myself, asking if he was looking for a guitar instructor.

"No," he replied, "are you the one from Maranatha! Music?"

"Yes, I'm one of the musicians with Maranatha."

"I need singers for a recording project, and they recommended you to me. Tell me more about your music background and ministry."

"Well, I have a music degree. I worked as a nightclub entertainer before God called me into music ministry with Calvary Chapel."

"That's great. So are you an alto or soprano?"

"Alto."

"I need to audition you," he said. "Could you sing 'Amazing Grace' for me right now, full voice?"

Over the phone? Okay. I stood there on the crowded boardwalk in my swimsuit and belted out the song for the whole world to hear.

I was in!

The following night, I arrived at Jimmy and Carol Owens' home to meet other musicians and vocalists. The Owens were innovators in contemporary Christian music. They had gathered us together to plan the recording of their new musical *Come Together*, narrated by Pat Boone. As we mingled and got acquainted, I spotted other Maranatha! musicians. I met Jimmy and Carol's fifteen-year-old daughter, Jamie, who was an up-and-coming Christian musician herself. I was also delighted to meet Buck and Annie Herring and Annie's younger sister and brother, Nellie and Matthew Ward. The three siblings had formed a contemporary Christian band called Second Chapter of Acts.

On the day we gathered to begin recording, I saw a hippie with long, bushy hair in the sound booth with Buck. When he sang with us the following day, I told someone I knew his voice from somewhere. "Oh," they said, "that's Barry McGuire." That blew me away! Barry was one of the lead vocalists in the popular '60s vocal group the New Christy Minstrels. I had learned and performed many of their songs, and Barry was one of my heroes! I didn't know he had become a Christian. *Wow, Lord*, I thought. *Very cool!*

Jimmy and Carol sat us down to explain the ministry they'd envisioned for their musical. "This musical is different," they said. "The audience is going to participate by praying with each other." There were interludes built into the musical that invited the audience to sing, participate, and pray. They called it "body ministry" or "body life" because folks couldn't just sit in the pews as spectators. Another element that was brand-new to me was singing in the Spirit. Amid the corporate worship, participants would be encouraged to sing their heartfelt worship songs, mingling harmoniously with others' spontaneous songs.

Most of our group were from a sizeable charismatic fellowship in Van Nuys called the Church on the Way, so this type of worship was familiar for them. But it was fresh and exhilarating to me. We began with prayer and sang in the Spirit during various parts of the recordings. Their openness to the Holy Spirit during recording sessions struck me. I carried that over into my future recording and mentoring experiences.

As a participant in the Owens' recording project, I rubbed shoulders with several people destined to become significant Christian music influences. Jimmy and Carol became my lifelong friends and mentors. I would have many opportunities to network with them in the coming years. God had strategically positioned me at the start of a coming tidal wave of contemporary Christian music and worship.

Musicians and ministries multiplied and thrived under the structure provided by Maranatha! Music. Children of the Day and Debby Kerner (later Kerner-Rettino) recorded the first individual ministry albums under the new label during the first year. Praise albums and testimonial albums such as *Maranatha 2* and *Maranatha 3* soon followed, involving various musicians.

Maranatha! Music's first Christian bands and single artists—Sweet Comfort Band, Love Song, Gentle Faith, Children of the Day, The Way, Debby Kerner, Mustard Seed Faith, Parable, Blessed Hope, Daniel Amos, Kelly Willard, Erick Nelson, Michele Pillar, and others—mostly played a mild folk-rock style of music. It gained acceptance as church music as young people everywhere started picking up the songs, passing them on, and making them popular. This music paved the way for a more radical music style on the horizon.

With so many musicians and new songs to choose from, the selection process for each Maranatha! Music project took prayerful consideration. It was an honor if they picked you for a project and even more to have one of your songs recorded. Because of how long I'd been with Maranatha! and my experience, I expected to be at the top of their list. But the Lord used this process to further test my motives and attitudes, aligning them with his purposes.

A new girl named Becky had been attending our meetings, and she sang like Joni Mitchell. I wasn't surprised when they included her on *Maranatha 3*, but I was shocked when I didn't appear on the list. It was a blow.

This seeming rejection bothered me so much I knew I had to take it to the Lord. As I did, I felt like God asked me why I wanted a song on the album. *Because I believe I have something to say*, I responded in my heart. *But if Becky's music speaks to people more powerfully than yours, then whose music should be on the album?* I cried. I knew what he was after. *Okay, Lord, I'll do what you want me to do. I guess I still have some growing to do.*

A couple of weeks later, I got a call from the office.

"Where's your song for *Maranatha 3*, Karen?"

"What song? My name wasn't on the list when you announced the musicians."

"Really?" they said in surprise. "We're sorry. Guess we just missed your name."

But I knew the truth. God had wanted to teach me something important about my priorities first. He had given me another opportunity to practice seeking him above my dreams and desires before fulfilling them for me. A few days later, I submitted the song "Plan of Love" for recording on *Maranatha 3.*

Maranatha! songs began to spread nationwide. Our leaders decided to record an album featuring praise music arising out of the Jesus movement. To my surprise and delight, they chose "Seek Ye First" to be on it. Peter Jacobs created a beautiful string arrangement for the song. I played guitar and oboe and sang a duet with Ernie Rettino. Completed in 1974, *The Praise Album* was a huge success. The album credits listed us as the Maranatha! Singers. People began calling to book us, not knowing we were a collection of individual musicians and bands, not a single group or a choir.

The simple song I wrote was now sung in churches and youth groups throughout Southern California and beyond. At first, it felt weird to hear others leading worship with "Seek Ye First." I was clueless about just how far it would travel and how important it would be to the future ministry God intended for me. That was just as well because God was still working on aspects of my character.

It seemed my identity hinged on whether I, my music, and my ministry cut it with Maranatha! Music's "in" crowd. There were particular people I wanted to associate with, but they didn't seem to be responding to me. I often cried over the sense of rejection I felt, and I didn't realize how much it had started to affect my outward appearance.

After a lunch concert at a university fellowship, one of their leaders called me to see if I was okay. "We were praying for you after you left," he told me. "You appear to be going through something."

I couldn't explain what it was. But I knew I needed to change, so I pressed into God.

Following a service one evening, Lonnie Frisbee led the After Glow gathering, inviting people to come to the front for prayer if they needed inner healing. *Well*, I thought, *I need healing of something*, so I went forward. As Lonnie prayed for me, I sensed the Lord speaking to me. *Karen, you're like a big apple tree, and your fruit, the fruit of the Spirit, is dropping. People are going by, and some are enjoying that fruit. But some don't even notice it. You're trying to shake your fruit off on them; you're trying to choose who you want to eat your fruit. Let me select the ones who need it and will eat the fruit naturally.*

The Lord showed me he had already put people in my life who wanted to be my friends, but they couldn't because I was trying to be friends with an exclusive group. From that point, I chose to befriend whomever God put in front of me. I also became friends with some of those I had been pursuing—without having to force it. I had been so insecure that I had missed the very point of "Seek Ye First." If I would seek him first and do his will, the bottom line was that he would bring his best to pass for me. If I depended on myself, disappointments would surely follow.

As the Jesus movement grew, so did the crowds. Our musicians faced new tests related to pride and financial stewardship. Our mentors believed in us, encouraging us to balance integrity and professionalism in our business dealings and to operate with Spirit-led creativity and compassion in our ministries. They released some Maranatha! bands and singers to make albums of their own. Recording an album was considered a result of genuine ministry, not a way to launch it.

Although Pastor Chuck was the father of Maranatha! Music, he always appointed someone else to be the manager. When I joined in 1971, that manager was Mike MacIntosh followed later by Chuck Fromm. The staff always felt like family to us. They served us in so many ways—marketing, publishing, artwork, sound production, warehouse management, and bookkeeping. Yet, it was not uncommon for them to stop their work to pray for one of us if they sensed a need.

Pastor Chuck and the leadership team would decide what songs would appear on the albums. Chuck also listened to the finished products before they were released. It was all about quality control, guidance, and releasing the kind of music and musicians that glorified God.

Late in 1973, I plucked up the courage to make an appointment with Pastor Chuck to ask about recording an album. I was nervous when I arrived at his office. *What if he thinks I want to do this because of pride? Lord, help me!*

I sat down in front of him, and as always, Chuck was relaxed and approachable. I began to recount my history with Maranatha! Music for him.

"Papa Chuck, you know I've been serving here a while, and I'm so thankful. I've played concerts regularly, written songs, and done some recording. I played oboe on *Maranatha 2* and guitar on *Maranatha 3*. They recorded one of my songs on that album. I was also a vocalist on Jimmy and Carol Owens' *Come Together* album. And now, my song, 'Seek Ye First,' has been selected for *The Praise Album*." Taking a deep breath, I plunged on. "Do you think it might be time for me to record my album?"

Chuck studied me. Then, in his typical, thoughtful way, he said:

"You have done some things, haven't you, Karen! Yes. Yes, I do think it's time for you to record your album." I was shocked. He picked up the phone and called Mike MacIntosh.

"Hi Mike," he said. "I'm here talking to Karen Lafferty, and I think it's time for her to record an album. Can you set things up?"

He scheduled the recording, and my first album, *Bird in a Golden Sky*, was released in 1975. It was a giant, validating step forward for me.

Over the next few years, many Maranatha! musicians became well-known and well-traveled. I soon launched out, too, doing music ministry in many little towns across the United States. I never aspired to be a Christian music superstar. I just loved traveling and singing for Jesus, especially in places where others might not go. While my friend Cathy Taylor sometimes handled my bookings during busy concert seasons, I was my ministry's primary steward. I booked myself in churches, prisons, and coffeehouses, playing in exchange for housing, meals, and a love offering. I also made a little money from album sales.

My small Toyota Chinook motor home became my second home.

Sometimes Maranatha! Music provided brochures, posters, bios, photos, and other marketing materials for their better-known ministries. I once asked them for some help with promotion and publicity, but it was not forthcoming, so I had to do most of it myself. Once again, I faced the temptation to wallow in self-pity, but I came to understand that I needed to trust God's call in my life and not expect others to do much of the work for me.

What I gleaned from my disappointment was good preparation for the future. Many musicians today look for a chance to get signed. They hope someone will do the work and make their way for them, including fame and fortune. However, if God has given them a vision, I tell artists they need to step out in obedience, not relying on others to do it for them. The trust-God attitude I developed working through my disappointments became the bedrock for years of ministry to come. The training I received in Maranatha! Music became the template by which I would disciple others.

CHAPTER 10

Beauty for Ashes

How would I know the feeling, how would I feel the pain,
If you always gave me sunshine, Lord, and I never felt the rain?
How would I know the sorrow, when you lose a child, you cry,
How it's hard to face tomorrow, you feel like part of you has died?
You feel like part of you has died.

—"Like a Morning Star" by Karen Lafferty, from *Sweet Communion*
© Capitol Christian Music Group

A s my touring increased, God brought me an unexpected friendship on the home front. Bobbi Walters was a bold, talented entertainer I met when I left the Moonraker. She came in with her agent right after I gave my notice, and she became my replacement. I occasionally stopped in at the restaurant to listen to her sing, and our friendship grew.

It soon became evident to me Bobbi had suffered significant hurts in life. She cried as she told me about her painful family life growing up, her rocky marriage and divorce, and the bitter custody battle over her young daughter that followed. Bobbi had been slandered because she had become an entertainer. That, coupled with a deceitful manipulation of the law, caused her to lose her little girl. It was almost more than she could take.

"Oh, Bobbi," I said. "I can tell that it is still excruciating for you. But I know God can heal those hurts if you give them to him. Would you please come to church with me?" She wiped her eyes and agreed to come.

Bobbi and I went to Calvary Chapel together, and before long, she raised her hand to receive the Lord during an altar call.

Bobbi's agent was disgusted when she heard she "got religion." They had a falling out, and soon Bobbi needed a place to live. Since I needed cheaper rent, we decided to get an apartment together in Orange County. We shared places for the next six years.

Bobbi struggled emotionally during much of that time, and I did my best to support her. When I returned home from one of my tours, she was experiencing abdominal pains. I took her to a doctor, knowing she had a history of cysts. When Bobbi returned to the waiting room after seeing the doctor, the staff handed her prenatal information. We looked each other in the eye. I had no idea she'd been with anyone, and I said, "Oh Lord, I wonder what you are going to do with this one."

It was a sober trip to the car, and we started for home in utter silence. Suddenly, Bobbi burst into tears and poured out her story. As it turned out, it was a one-time situation with a mutual friend.

"I'm so sorry, Karen. I never meant for this to happen." She paused and put her hands on her stomach. "I know this may sound strange, but I'm excited that I'm pregnant. I want to keep this baby. It's just that I don't feel I should marry the guy. But I *would* like him to be involved in the baby's life. You know," she continued softly, "this baby is a miracle. After I gave birth to my daughter, they told me I could never have another baby."

What could I say? "Well then, Bobbi, we'll just give this to God, and you know I'll support you any way I can."

Bobbi and I carved out space in our apartment for a baby room and made preparations to receive a newborn into our lives. I carried Bobbi emotionally through all the aches and pains of the pregnancy. It was the closest I've ever felt to giving birth to a child of my own.

Bobbi's little Tiffany, my first godchild, was born on August 12, 1974. She was healthy, pink-skinned, vibrant. Tiffany had wispy brown hair and big blue eyes, with a pretty streak of brown in one of them. I marveled at her plump, animated body and eager fingers. My love for Tiffany grew more each day as I helped feed and care for her. And as this good-natured, perfect baby girl grew, I was happy to know I was going to be involved in her life and future.

Bobbi's faith seemed to be growing even as her daughter grew. One Sunday after Thanksgiving, we went to church. We dedicated baby Tiffany to God as the father and friends gathered around. On December 13, when Tiffany was four months old, we went to church, and Bobbi left her in the nursery for the first time. Following the service, she said, "I know you're going to visit with a few people, so I'll go get Tiffany and wait for you in the car."

After I finished, I headed to the car, but Bobbi wasn't there. I waited and grew more concerned by the minute. I finally got out of the car and went back into the church. A crowd had gathered. I knew something was wrong.

"A baby has died," someone told me. I felt like I'd taken a punch in the stomach. *Oh God, don't let it be Tiffany.*

I elbowed my way through the crowd and into the nursery. There sat Bobbi, rocking in a chair and crying hysterically as the paramedics hovered over Tiffany's still form. Pastor Chuck and his wife, Kay, sat close beside Bobbi. The distressed nursery worker, pregnant herself, tried to explain, "Tiffany was just fine, but when I came over to recheck her later, she wasn't breathing."

The paramedics finished their work. Tiffany had died of sudden infant death syndrome (SIDS). They carried Tiffany's little body away without letting Bobbi hold her one last time. I mustered my strength, picked up the diaper bag, and helped Bobbi out to the car for the trip home.

Bobbi sank into a depression so deep I wondered how she could survive. Our apartment was prepped for a happy first Christmas and was full of baby things. The last photo I had taken of Tiffany was as she sat in a little bouncy chair under the tree. Packing away those baby things brought daily waves of grief to both of us; the clothes, toys, and baby paraphernalia represented so many dashed hopes and dreams. The closer it got to Christmas and the New Year, the harder it was to console Bobbi, even with the help of friends and a counselor.

Only God could heal a hurt this deep. And unbeknownst to me, Bobbi was calling out to the Lord in her despair, saying, "You have to do something. I can't take this!"

One afternoon, I returned from town and went to check on her.

"Are you okay?" I asked as I entered the room. As soon as I saw her, I knew something had happened. Peace and contentment had replaced her despair.

"Karen, I had a vision. Jesus was standing right there, in a light that was brighter and clearer than any I've ever seen," she said with quiet amazement, pointing to the foot of the bed. "He was smiling and holding Tiffany in his arms. She was happy and laughing! Do you know what he told me? He said, 'We'll all be together soon.'" For good measure, the Lord gave her the same vision again a few days later.

Bobbi rose from her bed that day, her depression gone. She was at complete peace with the knowledge that Tiffany was safe in the Lord's keeping. Not only that, she was full of grace and awe. God had accepted her, failures and all, and had heard and responded to her cries.

Tiffany died during the time I was recording my album *Bird in a Golden Sky*. When it was released the following year, I dedicated it to her. It also contained a song called "Bobbi's Song." In 1978, I released a second album with Maranatha! Music called *Sweet Communion*. In the years between the first album and this one, I suffered the loss of several other people I loved. A favorite aunt died of cancer. My talented Maranatha! Music friend Bill Sprouse died at age twenty-six. And my cousin Rock, who had introduced me to Calvary Chapel, took his own life through a drug overdose, unable to cope with flashbacks from his time in Vietnam. On top of Tiffany's untimely death, all these losses sent me reeling in grief and asking a lot of hard questions.

I began giving this pain to God through my songs, and I had many tearful moments recording them in the studio. The Holy

Spirit hovered over the production of *Sweet Communion*, as God used it to exchange the ashes of all my sorrow for his beauty. Of all the albums I've made, that one remains the most requested. I believe it's because the songs express heartfelt sadness and a hunger for God's comfort universal to us all. *Sweet Communion* is my most profound, most spiritual album—a testimony to our Father and our loved ones, who are never far away.

CHAPTER 11

Into All the World

We've a story to tell to the nations
That shall turn their hearts to the right,
A story of truth and mercy,
A story of peace and light.
We've a song to be sung to the nations
That shall lift their hearts to the Lord,
A song that shall conquer evil
And shatter the spear and sword.

—"We've a Story to Tell to the Nations" by H. Ernest Nichol (public domain), medley arrangement
©1983 Maranatha! Music as recorded in "Story Medley" by Karen Lafferty on *Country to Country*
© Capitol Christian Music Group

By the late 1970s, my ministry travels were shifting from the United States to other continents. God continued to chip away at my rough edges, reinforcing lessons that enhanced my ability to face challenging situations overseas. He used the open door of ministry to teach me how to reach out to people, nurturing a vision for using music as a tool in missions and evangelism.

In 1976, I toured Australia with the Maranatha! band, Phoenix Sonshine, led by Gary Cowan. We traveled from city to city in a short school bus, playing in churches, schools, shopping malls, even on board a US Navy ship. We also worked with the pastor and motorcycle rider, Dr. John Smith. He had founded a Christian motorcycle club called God's Squad, attracting riders the Australians referred to as "bikies." John was a gifted evangelist and Bible teacher who later influenced musicians like Bono and his band U2.

In addition to firing up my desire to evangelize, the Australian tour expanded my knowledge about honoring host cultures. In Melbourne, we stayed with missionaries who had served in Asia and were sponsoring our tour. In our youthful ignorance, we managed to do everything possible to abuse the privilege and offend them. Fortunately, they had the experience and good grace to sit us down and explain what we had done.

"You love the Lord and have a calling," they began, "but there are some things you need to learn about travel and ministry." They explained how we needed to value the differences between other cultures and ours. We had insulted them by insinuating America was better than Australia, saying things like "I'd give anything for an *American* hamburger." We made them feel awkward, disrespected, and unappreciated for all they had done to serve us. We also failed to treat their homes and possessions with respect. In short, we had been selfish, self-important, and ungrateful. It was embarrassing and eye-opening for me. We repented. Since then, I've tried to serve and practice cultural sensitivity wherever I find myself and have made it a priority to teach these things to the musicians I've mentored.

In the meantime, Maranatha! Music was developing into a professional record company under Chuck Fromm's leadership. The business included the overseas distribution of our albums. As a result, "Seek Ye First" was becoming known to an international audience.

Overseas distributors invited our musicians to come to their part of the world, and some from Europe specifically asked me. Maranatha! released me to go, and I began preparing for a three-month European tour, with stops in England, France, Germany, Austria, Switzerland, Belgium, and Holland. It also included a brief ten-day Calvary Chapel tour to Israel.

A month before the tour began, I played at a church in Orange County, where Floyd McClung Sr. was the pastor. His missionary son, Floyd Jr., spoke that evening. I sang my songs to open the meeting and then gave the floor to the younger McClung, who towered well over six feet in height and spoke in a deep, resonant voice. As soon as he began talking, I thought, *Wow! Who is this guy?*

A passionate love for Jesus and people blazed in his eyes. He was easygoing yet full of life and authority. I was captivated as he described his work with Youth With A Mission (YWAM) in Afghanistan. In Kabul, he and his wife Sally established the Dilaram House (*dilaram* is a Farsi word meaning "peaceful heart"). They worked with disillusioned young people trekking the infamous Hippie Trail from Amsterdam. They later moved to Amsterdam to begin working with needy young people there.

I knew little about YWAM, but Holland got my attention. The ministry center in Amsterdam where Floyd and Sally worked consisted of a couple of old houseboats located on the Ij River.

They were collectively dubbed the Ark. The name rang some bells—first because I realized I had been there and taken photos of the Ark when I toured with Children of the Day five years earlier. And second, because it included a coffee bar ministry—the same kind of ministry that had caught my interest at coffeehouse in New Orleans. The whole thing intrigued me, and it seemed like a perfect venue to squeeze into my itinerary.

After the meeting, I approached Floyd and introduced myself, explaining that I would be in Europe the next month on a concert tour, and could I please come and visit?

"Yes! Please visit! We have hospitality rooms where you can stay. Here's our location and how to get in touch."

God had just masterminded a divine appointment for me. Once I arrived in Europe, he would start the process of rerouting my life.

When I arrived alone in Europe, I was faced right away with the familiar battle of loneliness. I was excited about the new ministry opportunities, but I wished someone else had come with me. Although people treated me well, I felt uneasy entering new surroundings by myself. Typically, my hosts and audiences did not speak English, and before long, I was homesick. In response, I did my best to press into God.

A friend had given me a little book titled *Come Away My Beloved* by Frances J. Roberts, which became my close companion. It provided precious revelation about fellowship that helped me to mature through those days. As my loneliness slowly transformed into a thoughtful solitude, I gained a new perspective on relationships.

I began to think of fellowship in terms of a triangle, with God at the topmost point. My Christian brothers and sisters are at one of the two bottom points, and I, as an individual, am at the remaining point. As we all move closer to the throne of God through prayer and fellowship, the distance between us diminishes. God gave me a vision of this in which I saw him comforting me in one arm and my family and friends in the other. I shared it with my sisters and mom, and we resolved to read the Word and pray at the same hour each day wherever we were. This practice closed the gap between us each time we met at God's throne in an hour of sweet, life-giving fellowship.

As I traveled throughout Europe, I often played in the same kind of small, out-of-the-way settings I loved in the United States. I discovered just how well known "Seek Ye First" had become in Europe. When I landed in Amsterdam, a television crew from the EO (*Evangelische Omroep*—Evangelical Broadcasting) met me. They sought an interview with me due to my song's popularity with Christians in Holland. In Belgium, three Catholic sisters slipped me a note saying they wanted to give me something during the concert. "Sisters," I said, "I hear you have something for me." They stood, looked at each other with a smile, and sang "*Cherchez de bor le reume de Dieu . . .*" I recognized the melody and knew they were singing "Seek Ye First" in French. What a blessing!

The contemporary Christian music that was exploding in America was a new thing in Europe. This fact became evident in Stier, Austria, where my performance took place in a beautiful, three-tiered concert hall. The hall was a venue for great orchestras and operas and choirs singing classic hymns. I felt insecure stepping out on that stage alone, with just my guitar, before an audience that spoke little English. "Seek Ye First" was the only song I had learned to sing in German. I was still learning how to work with a translator and overhead transparencies.

I probably amuse these people, I thought as I played. *They'll soon be bored.* I decided to sing songs special to me, like the ones about my grandmother's faith and birds in a golden sky. I did my best to communicate through my interpreter. I hoped my songs would speak to the young people in the audience, but their expressions told me nothing. To my surprise, the audience stayed with me for the entire hour and a half. I think they had never heard Christian songs written about such things before.

I left that night thinking I had not been very effective. It wasn't until after I finished the tour and returned to the United States that I received numerous letters from my Austrian sponsors. They told me the folks from Stier were still talking about the concert! They passed my album around, and people were still getting saved—just from listening to the album and talking about the lyrics! Despite the language barrier, God used me in a place where people had never experienced anything like my ministry or music. He also reminded me that *he* spoke German, French, and Dutch very well.

Throughout Europe, I saw how the American entertainment industry had done me a favor as a Christian musician. People around the world were listening to the same folk and pop style of music. They all had heard the Beatles. They could sing along on

John Denver's "Country Roads." I could sing Carole King's music and people related to it. The exposure to and familiarity with contemporary music paved a broad highway for me to play similar music styles but with a different message.

Young people would approach me after my concerts to ask how they could serve the Lord as musicians. I didn't know what to tell them other than to help in their churches. But then God opened my eyes to another possibility. At some of my concerts, I met Americans and Europeans involved with YWAM, the ministry I had heard about from Floyd McClung. Most of these "YWAMers" could speak both English and the local language. It occurred to me that there might be among them a woman interested in traveling with me and translating for me in host homes and concerts. That person could then share about ministry opportunities available through Youth With A Mission. YWAM leaders embraced the idea, which was another positive thing that drew me to the organization.

I kept a journal throughout the Europe tour. In many places I'd been, I was the first American pop/folk artist they'd heard singing about Jesus. I wrote, *Why aren't we going out to the places no one is going? Why aren't we doing more of this all around the world? What an incredible tool this kind of music ministry would be to reach young people everywhere!*

I knew it wouldn't be enough to do an occasional tour; Christian artists needed to get fully involved. But how? I wrote down my new vision and what it might look like if put into action, all the while thinking, *If only someone would start a program or a school to help musicians get into missions, then I could help.* What I hadn't considered was that God might be asking *me* to get the ball rolling.

I had scheduled four free days in Holland to visit YWAM Heidebeek, where Floyd McClung Jr. served as leader. I was eager to meet other young people who were working as missionaries. I caught the train to Heerde, where a young YWAMer picked me up at the station. As we drove through the picturesque Dutch countryside and onto the YWAM Heidebeek property, I was charmed right away.

As soon as we arrived, their hospitality staff welcomed me and took me to a pleasant guest room in a large house. The building had several bedrooms for staff and students and a classroom for their Discipleship Training School (DTS). The table in my room had a welcome basket. They had filled it with snacks, a welcome card, and books filled with mission stories (including *Just Off Chicken Street*, which Floyd had written about his work in Afghanistan). One of YWAM's Foundational Values is hospitality. Right away, I felt welcome and at home.

While at Heidebeek, I took many walks and bike rides through the beautiful forest surrounding the area, discovering the heather fields from which Heidebeek takes its name. One morning, Floyd asked me to give the staff and students a concert during their regular "family time." He gave me the whole hour, which was a tremendous honor, for this was a necessary meeting time for their missions community. God was already bonding me to the YWAM family!

One evening, Floyd and Sally invited me for dinner in their cozy apartment, and I shared what I had observed on my tour from my journal. "Christian music ministry saturates America, yet there is so little of it and so much opportunity here in Europe."

"What are you proposing?" Floyd asked.

"Young people in Europe are interested in contemporary Christian music. I think we need to use music in missions!"

I laid out ideas about how effective it could be to bring musicians and bands in to do evangelism.

"If God can use even an insecure foreigner like me, I believe he will use other young musicians to reach this generation. If there are opportunities to use music in missions, I believe lots of Christian musicians will respond."

A few days later, Floyd approached me to say, "I've been praying about your vision, and I feel it's of God. If you want us to help you with it, let me know." Wow! I'd never had any leader say they were praying about *my* vision. It gave me a lot to think about—this could be the way to get some of my musician friends at home involved in world missions.

After my wonderful retreat at Heidebeek, I traveled to Amsterdam to see where the YWAMers were ministering. They took me to the Ark, the two houseboats next to the city's busy Central Train Station. One of the boats housed YWAM staff. They transformed the other into a long, open coffee bar with patchwork carpeting, lounge pillows, power line spools made into tables, and hanging ceiling lights draped with paisley scarves. If I hadn't known it was a Christian ministry, I would have thought it was a drug house!

A stool and a small sound system sat against one wall, and I was the program for the evening. The audience consisted of both American and European hippies (most of whom could speak English). It was the perfect setting for my storytelling ballads. The kind of place Jesus would be found, talking with the people. Many who came to the Lord through the Ark's ministry went on to do discipleship training at Heidebeek.

I finished my European tour and headed home, eager to explore the potential of involving musicians in missions. I talked to Maranatha! leaders, Jimmy and Carol Owens, and anyone who would listen concerning what I thought we *ought* to be doing. Everyone thought it was a great idea; after all, it was the Great Commission. But at that time, none could commit to helping me pursue the vision.

Then I remembered Floyd's invitation. I realized my new passion for helping musicians move into effective international ministry could take wing through YWAM. Although I didn't know much about the mission, I took what Floyd said seriously. I decided YWAM was the route to go.

At the same time, it dawned on me that this might be the answer to how a musician could secure the necessary financial support to pursue ministry. After I went from entertainment to ministry, I was still a professional musician, but I made less money. I had to live on whatever I could make from album sales, royalties, and occasional offerings. But because churches sent missionaries out and helped them financially, being involved in missions as a musician made financial sense.

I knew if I were going to work with Floyd, I would have to relocate to Holland. I started booking a second concert tour to

Europe, planning to attend a Discipleship Training School at Heidebeek afterward. From there, I would launch my new vision "to go where no Christian musician had ever gone before."

CHAPTER 12

A New Horizon—
Youth With A Mission

I could be waking up one day
To your sun on an Asian sea.
Father, you'd be there that day
To speak your love to me.
Or I could walk along a Dutchman's path,
Feel your Spirit on the Zuider Zee,
And I could meditate there
On your oceans of love for me.

—"With You" by Karen Lafferty, from *Country to Country*
© Capitol Christian Music Group

I returned to YWAM Heidebeek in the fall of 1979 to participate in their Discipleship Training School (DTS). God had been shaping me through my Baptist roots, Campus Crusade, and Calvary Chapel. Now I was crossing another spiritual threshold—so significant that YWAM would become my permanent "tribe."

I didn't realize at the time that I was entering the ranks of one of the most progressive and far-reaching mission organizations in existence. Loren and Darlene Cunningham founded YWAM in 1960. YWAM's motto is "to know God and to make Him known," a calling it accomplishes through training, evangelism, and mercy ministries. The Cunninghams rocked the traditional church's mission paradigm by training and sending thousands of young believers to proclaim Jesus worldwide. Other YWAM ministry methods were also considered revolutionary at the time: a live-learn model of discipleship, the belief that every faithful Christian can hear God's voice, emphasis on short-term, cross-cultural outreaches, and the idea that people from every nation can be missionaries.

The faith and familiarity I experienced at Maranatha! Music provided a perfect entrée into this new world of global opportunities. YWAM welcomed fresh vision, and I envisioned myself helping raise and release musicians from many nations into international ministry.

I considered myself spiritually mature. But the DTS (now offered in many countries and languages) showed me how much I still had to learn about the ways of God. The five-month school consists of three months in the classroom and two months on outreach. It ensures that all potential YWAM missionaries receive the same foundational training in living a faithful, joyful, prayerful, Christlike life. I learned to confront areas of personal pain and sin, how to wait on God and hear his voice, and how to pray as I had never prayed before. I also learned to appreciate other cultures and to be flexible in any situation I found myself in. This practical, daily application of God's Word as a lifestyle was essential as God continued to shape me into what he wanted me to be.

Part of YWAM's ethos is to learn as you go, and living in a community—eating, sleeping, working, and playing together— is how we practiced and prepared for missions. About eighty students and staff in my DTS, from eight different nations, lived in close quarters on a tight budget. Working out the things they taught us challenged me to maintain a servant's heart and accountability to others.

We came from different countries, denominations, careers, and social groups and focused simply on becoming one in Jesus. I took off my musician's hat for a season to embrace what the Lord was going to do in me as I sought to be a true disciple. In the classroom, we faced our need for grace and forgiveness, explored what it meant to be transparent before God and each other, and learned how to pray for different cultures and peoples. On a practical level, they assigned each student a work duty, such as assisting in the kitchen, cleaning, doing yard work, and other necessary chores. My work duty was helping with laundry.

Our lean school budget didn't allow for luxuries. Still, we held "love feasts" every Friday night, where we gathered for fellowship over a special meal. Our usual diet consisted of rice or pasta dishes with a bit of meat. But for love feasts, we dressed up and sat down to cloth-covered tables and candlelight, each of us receiving a whole serving of meat with our dinner along with coffee and dessert. After the meal, we worshiped God together with thankfulness.

On Monday nights, I attended my small group's weekly meeting at the home of our leaders, Ron and Roberta Archer. They understood the importance of building loving relationships and nurtured us with prayer, teaching, fellowship, and delicious desserts.

My Heidebeek roommate was a staff member from New Zealand named Christine. I was a little older than Christine, but she was a mature prayer warrior. She influenced my life with her prophetic gifting and servant heart. Each chilly night, she warmed my bed in advance by tucking a "hottie" (hot water bottle) under the covers with my pajamas wrapped around them.

Heidebeek is a Dutch farm community nestled in the beautiful Veluwe area of Holland. During our time off, our students walked or biked through the nearby forests. There was no movie theater or urban entertainment nearby, but we found other satisfying things to do. We read together, watched movies, played games, and shared stories for hours.

As students of YWAM Heidebeek, initiation into some of the Dutch people's customs and routines came naturally. Something profound happened in us just living among people of different ideals and traditions. Between the YWAM and Dutch cultures, my values and sense of tradition grew deep and rich— foundational preparation for the call God had in store for me.

Once we finished the lecture (teaching) phase of our DTS, we headed out to practice what we had learned. My outreach team drove to Athens, Greece, where we would join eight other

DTS teams (a total of about two hundred students) at a single campground.

It was a hot, sweaty, five-day drive without showers and with few restroom stops. The bus broke down in a small town in Yugoslavia, and while it was under repair, some of us girls spotted a coffee shop. We ordered small cups of espresso, meant to be sipped slowly. However, I didn't know that, and I gulped coffee sludge that left me choking and sputtering. The café patrons—all men—got a good laugh out of my misery!

Our first overnight stay in Greece was at a camp near Mount Olympus. We arrived late and set up our tents in the dark. In the morning, I opened the flap of my tent and saw the Aegean Sea. I was awestruck, thinking *Paul could have walked here!* By the time we boarded the bus for the next leg of the journey, a new song I had titled "Aegean" was already brewing in my mind.

The next day we settled at the Varkiza campground outside of Athens. Our leaders began praying and planning our outreach in the area. One of the first things the Lord spoke to them was that we must be sensitive to the culture, beginning with our appearance. Many of our guys had long hair and beards—one had a beard that reached his waist. Only the Orthodox priests wore beards in Greece, and our leaders felt our guys should cut their beards so they wouldn't offend anyone. Some had had their beards for years. "It won't be difficult," the leaders said, "unless your hair has grown so long that it has grown into your heart." All the guys agreed to do it and took pictures before and after to mark the occasion.

Our routine consisted of going out every day to share the Lord with people. One DTS team performed an evangelistic drama called *Toymaker and Son*. In this drama, a toymaker creates beloved toys, placing them in a land where they can live in a safe and happy relationship with him. But when an evil apprentice leads the toys away from the toymaker into corruption and misery, the toymaker sends his only son to redeem them and bring them back. As the team dramatized this allegory, the rest of us went out into the crowds to witness.

One day, the police shut us down (for unknown reasons), so our leaders prayed about what to do next. They divided us into groups of about fifteen and sent us around the city to pray. Guitars in hand, my teammates and I formed a circle in a parking lot and began singing, praying, and worshiping. We soon attracted a crowd without intending to do so. Our leader, John Goodfellow, stepped forward and began speaking.

"You might wonder who we are," he began. "We're a group of Christian students from all over the world. We're worshiping in different languages, and we've come to pray for Greece and Athens and to share the love of Christ." He then explained the simple gospel, approaching them as citizens of a God-fearing nation and talking about how God wants to be involved in their daily lives. He closed by saying, "If you need prayer, come forward, and we will pray for you."

And they came. I thought of Psalm 40:3, where David says, "He hath put a new song in my mouth, even praise unto our God: many shall see it, and fear, and shall trust in the LORD" (KJV).

On another occasion, hundreds gathered while we ministered. As one of our Heidebeek DTS students, Steve Boston, spoke about the love of God, a huge Greek man wearing a flat cap pushed his way through the crowd. The man marched right up

Family

Walter

Ollie and Walter Lafferty

Ollie

"Big Jim" Lafferty

Jamettie Lafferty

Sam and Satie Stout

Karen, age 3

Karen and Fran
learning piano

Christmas, 1954: Walter Jr., Ollie, Walter Sr., Fran, Karen, Satie

Paul and Ollie Brown, Jerry, Karen, and Fran at home in
Alamogordo, 1963

Stepbrother
Jerry Brown

Paul and Ollie Brown

Satie and Gary Hamberg, 2018

Fran and Monty Bunker family, 1974

Walter and Margaret Lafferty, 2011

Paul, Ollie, and the five kids

Family fun

Cowgirl Karen

Grandma Stout and Ollie with Karen,
winner of local Ruidoso pageant, first runner
up in 1970 Miss New Mexico pageant

Fran and Karen with Daddy

Karen and Daddy at White Sands

The Sundowners: Bobbye Buttram, Annette
Zimmerman, and Karen

Grandma Stout playing the musical saw

University and Entertaining Years

The Joyful Noise, 1967:
Karen, Bob and Jerry Jones

Karen the cancan dancer (in gold),
The Unsinkable Molly Brown

USO Tour, 1968: Greenland, Iceland,
Labrador (Canada)

Opera excerpt from *Così fan tutte* (Karen on left)

USO number: "Hey, Big Spender"

Club entertaining, 1970

All-Campus Sing trophy
for the Zeta Tau Alpha
Sorority

Jesus Movement Years

Pastor Chuck and Kay Smith

Maranatha! Music concert, 1978

The Calvary Chapel tent, 1973

First "Seek Ye First"
sheet music, 1975

Recording: Jonathan David Brown (producer),
Kelly Willard, Becky Ugartechea, Karen

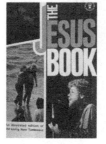

Jesus movement
Bible

Publicity shot

Maranatha! Music retreat, 1977

Mentors Jimmy and Carol Owens

Beach baptisms at Pirate's Cove, Corona del Mar
(2 photos)

Maranatha! Music logo

Publicity shot

Night of Joy
concert, Disneyland

Publicity shot

Holland

YWAM Heidebeek

A YWAM "love feast"

Samaritan's Inn,
Amsterdam

The Ark, Amsterdam

De Poort, YWAM training building

Amsterdam canals

Eddie Huff, first MFM director, 1982

Musicians for Missions (MFM) staff, 1982: Karen, Naomi Boshoff, Celeste Yohai, Steve Basler

Karen with Ria and Leen LaRiviére, Christian Artists Seminar Europe leaders

Karen with YWAM Amsterdam leaders Floyd and Sally McClung (2 photos)

Musicians Summer of Service (MSOS), 1982

How we travel in Holland

MFM bands on the streets of Amsterdam, 1980s
(top two photos)

MFM International, 1991

MFM and YWAM Holland staff, 1984

Publicity shot

Musicians Summer of Service bands

The band Lazarus on the
MV Anastasis (Mercy Ships)

Konsert voor de Koning (Concert for the King), 1986

Tours

Karen, Belinda, and Janet at the
Berlin Wall, East Germany and
Poland tour, 1990

Summer band in Budapest, Hungary, 1993

Working with Romanian choirs
and songwriters, 1992

Romanian hymnist Nicolae Maldoveanu

South Africa anti-apartheid rally, 1990

Christian Artists South Africa with artists Bobby Michaels, Scott Wesley Brown, Elly & Rikkert (Holland), the Mulders (S. Africa), and the Boshoffs (directors)

Christian Music Academy, Nigeria, 2017

Aids conference in Zimbabwe

Alsace, France, tour with Kjell-Håkon (Norway), Lotta (Denmark), Karen (USA), Jocelyne (France), and Daniel (France)

Karen in traditional Alsation dress

Romanian tour, 2003: Ruth Herrera,
Farrah McLuhan, Karen

Italy tour, 1990: Angela Diprima, Karen,
Christine Reymond, Marie McKenzie

Receiving gifts after a school concert
in Thailand, 2017

India music school performance, 2015:
Joyce Meade, Karen, and Minions

Honduras, 2013
Our host, Jennifer
Bullock, Corazon
de Dios Ministry

First Baptist Santa Fe team

Karen singing for Honduran children

International Festival of the Arts
Kunming, China, 2004: Native Americans
and Chinese indigenous people

Olympics

Sydney 2000 Olympics outreach team

Sydney Opera House

London 2012 Olympics, Eyes Open band (2 photos)

London 2012 Olympics outreach team

Schools

First School of Music in Missions (SOMM) in Amsterdam (eight nations represented), 1995

SOMM poster

College of **Arts & Sports**

Santa Fe SOMM outreach:
Christmas Around the World (2 photos)

Loren and Darlene
Cunningham, founders
of YWAM and
University of the Nations

Mentors Colin Harbinson,
David Garrett

College of Arts & Sports
leadership committee

Karen and Benny Prasad,
SOMM India leaders

First SOMM in India, 2001

Music Ministry Development Seminar,
Discover Bay, Washington, 2013

Sabo (Nigeria) recording

Santa Fe

YWAM Santa Fe pioneering staff, 1997:
Sandy and Julia Hoffman and children,
Barbara Choina, Karen

MFMI leadership team, 1999

First big event: *Feliz Navidad* New Mexico with Fernando Ortega, 1998 (2 photos)

Christian Musician Summit:
Chad and Meagen Moody at
the MFMI booth

Art and Missions tour: Marianne Millar (visual artist),
Jennifer Bullock (photographer), Karen (musician)

Producing a CD in the Towa language (2 photos)

Karen's ordination,
Calvary Chapel Las Vegas,
New Mexico, 2018

Recordings

Karen's first recording,
1966

First recording of
"Seek Ye First," 1974

"Seek Ye First"
sheet music, 1977

1975

1978

1980

1982

MFM compilation album,
1986

1989

1995

2003

2008

to Steve, grabbed him by the shoulders, and gave him a big kiss. Everyone cheered as the man turned and walked away.

Steve was surprised but continued sharing until another man in the audience interrupted him.

"Are you saying we can know God personally?" the man asked.

"Yes," Steve replied. "That's what I'm saying. God wants us to know him as our Father."

"Well, I'm a teacher of theology at the University of Athens," the man said, "and I want to talk to you." The gathering broke up soon after that, but many collected around Steve and the professor, wanting to hear what Steve had to say. The professor thought we were Jehovah's Witnesses, and after Steve explained to him we were not, the man said,

"You're an evangelist, aren't you?"

"I guess so," Steve replied. The man turned to the crowd with great excitement.

"God has brought an evangelist to Athens!" he shouted. The people got excited too! Turning back to Steve, he said, "I want you to come and speak to my class."

It was thrilling to go out every day and share the gospel. I thought of Paul's missionary trip to Athens and how the Greeks loved talking about new things and ideas. In all those years, the Greeks hadn't changed; people still gathered in city squares and parks, gesturing and talking. On Easter, we prayed and shared on Mars Hill. Paul had preached there before an altar inscribed "To The Unknown God" (Acts 17:23 KJV). And here we were, like Paul, declaring the truth about the Lord.

Outreach was not just about seeing God move when we were out on the streets. It was also a time to see God move in our hearts, as we encountered inevitable challenges. For me, who had been a bit of a spoiled kid, it was an opportunity to trust God for my daily bread. Though I had money in the bank, I hadn't been able to cash a check for weeks, so I was penniless. That meant I couldn't go out for coffee and baklava with friends. Also, with so many of us to feed at the camp, we sometimes ran out of food. There was always bread for latecomers, so some days I lived on only bread and water.

There were many women in the camp and only four showers, so it was hard to find a good time to bathe. One morning, I awoke just before dawn and hurried to the showers, thinking I would be able to beat the others. I arrived to find many girls already standing in line, so I walked up the hill to watch the beautiful sunrise over the Aegean Sea. I went far enough away from the camp so as not to be heard, and there, feeling free, I began singing, "Lord, I'll go anywhere for you." Then I stopped. *Wow. Would I do that?*

I thought of the friends I had recently made who were leaving the next day to work in some new and dangerous Cambodian refugee camps. *Would I be willing to do something like that,* I wondered? God spoke to me at that moment, saying, *I will never leave you. I will be with you wherever you go for me.* I understood then that I would be at home with the Lord wherever I was.

While we may already know such truths, God uses moments like that to make them truly ours. That morning, he said to me, *Whenever you feel weak, get up and watch the sunrise.* During a trip to India some years later, I got a similar reminder. As I got off a plane and descended the steps, I saw palm trees and slum shanties silhouetted against the red-orange sunrise. Suddenly, a blast of heat and stench made me wonder what I was doing there. Then I remembered God was there with me.

The third time God spoke to me through a sunrise was as I was flying out of Santa Fe, New Mexico, one morning. The sun was rising over the Sangre de Cristo Mountains, painting them red. It was so beautiful I wanted to shout, "Look at that, everybody!" As I communed with God there on the plane, he spoke this into my heart: *I am the God of Abraham, Isaac, and Jacob; and of your mom, and your Grandma Stout.* The list went on. *I have put eternity in their hearts and connected you to eternity.* What an astounding revelation! I was connected to eternity and my loved ones by the eternal God!

Like so many other experiences he has orchestrated in my life, my encounter with God that morning in Greece further convinced me of his love, holiness, and righteousness. I could only think: *How can I not serve the Lord? How could I embrace any other life or belief?*

CHAPTER 13

Worldview, Heart View

"When you forgive, you love. And when you love,
God's light shines upon you."

—Jon Krakauer, *Into the Wild*

T he Discipleship Training School experience helped me see the world with fresh eyes. First, I learned to understand and appreciate other cultures at a deeper level. Until the DTS, I didn't realize how much my American worldview influenced my thinking. Second, the training allowed the Holy Spirit to expose places in my heart that still needed his healing touch.

I decided to stay in Holland after my DTS, making it my home base for the next sixteen years. I am so grateful for my education in Holland's wonderful culture during that time. Most people get to see other countries only as visitors. It was my privilege to learn their language and live among them.

I undertook a five-month immersion program in the Dutch language, history, and culture. I stayed with two different families, Piet and Mari Knol and Wil and Ineke Oskam and their children. Although these couples knew English, they would not speak a word of it to me. I woke up daily rehearsing phrases like *"Mag ik het brood, alsjeblieft?"* which means "May I have the bread, please?"

In these Christian home settings, I fell in love with a family-centered tradition. Once the mother had placed the food on the table, everyone seated themselves for the evening meal. The father would give thanks to God and then say, *"Eet smakelijke,"* which means "Eat deliciously." After dinner, he or one of the children would get out the family Bible and read a few verses. They typically followed up the reading with discussion and a closing prayer. The children and their father then washed and dried the dishes together.

I discovered significant differences between my American culture and the Dutch culture. For instance, many Americans guard themselves against speaking what is on their mind. But the Dutch are pretty blunt. Many say things the way they see them, not thinking about how it may make others feel. Words and expressions also differ in meaning between our two languages. For example, when the Dutch say, *"Hij is een kennis,"* they're saying "he is an acquaintance," not a friend. Dutch folk don't call anyone a friend unless there is a genuine relationship between them. On the other hand, Americans often call someone a friend even if they've only met once.

I came to love many Dutch traditions. Their pride in neatness. Their practice of keeping fresh flowers on their tables. Their habit of taking a gift of wine and chocolate—and their friendship—to bless their hosts.

I especially loved the Dutch *gezelligheid* (for which there is no equivalent English word). *Gezelligheid* is the cozy, welcoming atmosphere created through daily fellowship intervals over tea or coffee made the Dutch way—strong and wonderful. It's a time of conversation and unhurried friendship. The Dutch live for the togetherness of these breaks taken like clockwork throughout the day, both at home and work. We maintained the *gezelligheid* in our YWAM community, stopping three times daily for tea, coffee, and fellowship. This intimate ritual profoundly affected me, and I have included it in my hospitality practices since then.

YWAM encourages its staff and students to study and value other cultures. In my experience, the best way to do that is to immerse yourself in your host culture. *All* the cultures and people who have hosted me over the years have enriched my life. I've sought to pass on my love and respect for other cultures to all those I mentor.

The most eye-opening experience of my DTS came about when God pried open a locked door in my heart. As I sat in class and listened to the teaching, I had a shocking revelation of how many people I held grudges against or had wronged. I had a history of hurt and rejection going back to my childhood, which subtly infected my relationships, especially with men. The Lord initiated a healing process during my DTS that continued for years. Initially, things got a lot worse, but my whole attitude and approach toward people shifted in a healthy, significant way. The process began with forgiving my stepfather, Paul.

It's one thing to talk about forgiveness and another thing to live it out. I realized I not only needed to forgive Paul for *not* being a father to me but for not knowing *how* to be one. I had thought of him mainly as a problem in my life, but God began by showing me how little I knew about this man.

Paul had worked for and socialized with my parents for years before Daddy died. He knew all about the Lafferty clan. I had rarely asked questions about his family background. I knew he was from Indiana and had been overshadowed in the service by a successful older brother. I knew he had been in the military and couldn't fulfill his dream of becoming a pilot due to physical issues. What I didn't realize was how these, or other events, might have shaped his character. He may not have been a bad person at all— he just came into our family at a time when I saw any replacement for my father as bad. My immaturity had caused me to respond in anger toward him, and that pattern continued for years.

My lesson from God didn't stop at just forgiving Paul. I had to come to grips with the root of my bitterness, get rid of it, and begin building a genuine relationship. I could no longer get by just tolerating him. The difficulty was that I didn't even know how to act around him. When Paul said things that touched a sore spot, I responded like the old Karen. Then I would get mad at myself. It fell to me to initiate a repair of our relationship because I knew he didn't know how. I needed a strategy.

I asked the Lord for a plan for Paul. He said: *Be interested in Paul Brown. Get to know the details of his life, and don't be afraid to touch him, to show him you care.*

In the years that followed, I made every effort to find ways to bless and honor him. Applying a DTS principle, I practiced responding to him in the opposite spirit whenever we clashed. I tried to respond to anger with calmness, arguments with listening, and stubbornness with humility. Not only did this work, but it also prevented our conflicts from escalating.

I often asked Paul about himself and his family, showing interest and paying him compliments. He suffered from bad headaches, so I volunteered to rub his neck and shoulders whenever I was around. Simple human touch ministered to him, opening the door to sincere conversations that deepened our bond.

One day, quite by accident, I learned something about Paul that helped me see him in a new light. He had never taken the initiative to come and see me perform. I got the feeling he disapproved of me being a musician. He once described my music career as "unstable." He never seemed supportive of my work. Then I ran into a friend on the street in Ruidoso who had worked with Paul.

He said, "I've heard a lot about your music ministry. Your stepdad talks about you all the time at work."

"He does?"

"Yes. Paul even shared some of your recordings with other coworkers and me."

He must have seen the shock in my eyes. Up until then, I had no idea that Paul was proud of me! I wondered what else I had taken personally or misinterpreted because I thought he didn't care.

One Christmas, my siblings and I surprised Mom and Paul with a trip to Holland to visit me. It was a big thing for them because they'd never been to Europe. During their visit, I took them out to a lovely Dutch restaurant. As we ate our dinner, I asked Paul about his grandparents. Paul expressed a fondness for them.

Then he told us a wrenching story about his elderly grandmother that left us all in tears.

"My family decided to send her to a nursing home because they couldn't take care of her. I was elected to take her there—and leave her. I was the only one who ever went to see her." He began to sob, crying so hard his tears dripped into his dinner plate. Even my mom was shocked; I don't think she had ever seen him so broken. I put my arm around him, acknowledging his pain and thanking him for sharing his story.

It turned out Paul was terrified that if my mom died, we would abandon him the same way his family had left his grandmother. "You've been my father for thirty-five years," I assured him. "You're part of our family, Paul, and you'll always be with us."

I persisted in doing what I could to build his trust, but Paul's fear ran deep. He said that he would have a nest egg to take care of himself if he ever got thrown out. He always carried a money clip full of hundred-dollar bills, and he stashed thousands in a bank account, "just in case."

After my mother passed away and Paul grew too frail to live alone, I did my best to honor him and the promise I'd made. By then, I was back in New Mexico, living in Santa Fe, so I moved him into my home. Paul stayed with me until the end. My sister Fran and my friend Bobbi stepped in to help whenever I was away in his last months. One night, sometime after I had said my goodbyes and left for India, he took one last drag on a cigarette, went to bed, and never woke up.

I'm glad we had developed a good relationship before he died. I think we finally convinced him he was part of the family.

Corrie ten Boom has always been one of my heroes. She was a Dutch Christian woman who helped Jewish people survive World War II and ended up in a concentration camp herself. I heard her speak on forgiveness once in my early years at Calvary Chapel. She testified about making the difficult choice to forgive the concentration camp guard responsible for her sister's death. Comparing unforgiveness to the pull rope on a big church bell, she explained how the rope gives the bell energy. Once we let go of the rope, the bell might ring a few more times, but it will eventually stop. Choosing against bitterness is like letting go of the rope. It silences the bell of pain and unforgiveness. Once I decided to forgive Paul—and others—that bell finally stopped in my life.

CHAPTER 14

Musicians for Missions

The Musician's Commission:
"Praise the LORD in song, for He has done glorious things;
let this be known throughout the nations."

—Isaiah 12:5 (NASB)

O nce I saw how God could use contemporary Christian music in missions, I was eager to enlist others. My discipleship and outreach experiences at Calvary Chapel and YWAM provided a ready-made template for my envisioned ministry. I called it Musicians for Missions (MFM). What I needed most to get it started were support staff and other musicians.

Steve and Lynn Basler, a staff couple from Heidebeek, were the first to join me in launching the vision. In 1980, I returned to Costa Mesa, California, to spend six months recruiting for our first Music Ministry School (MMS), scheduled for the following summer. My first recruit from Calvary Chapel was Celeste Yohai. She later came on MFM staff and still works as a missionary in Amsterdam today.

Even though MFM was born out of a vision and calling God had given me, I didn't want to lead it. I preferred to work alongside others under a strong leader. I began asking God for a director. I found that in Eddie Huff.

I met Eddie on my recruiting trip when I spoke at the Jesus Chapel in El Paso, Texas. He invited me to perform at a Christian music festival he was organizing in the city. I agreed to come. The festival didn't bring enough income to cover expenses, and Eddie felt terrible that he couldn't pay me the promised honorarium. I wrote him a letter to forgive the debt and felt led to tell him about Musicians for Missions. I explained the vision and invited him to pray about coming to help. To my surprise, he replied quickly, saying, "We're coming!"

Eddie said he'd been thinking about studying law, but God spoke to him to change direction after reading my letter. He was especially interested in MFM's European connection because his mother was German and his father was African American. As a German-speaking person, it had always been in Eddie's heart to minister in the country of his birth. He packed up his wife and two children and headed to Holland to do a DTS.

Eddie had tremendous administrative and managerial skills and a heart for and understanding of musicians. After his DTS, he stepped into the role of "prime minister" of Musicians for Missions. He said I was its "queen," and he nicknamed me Queenie. For four fruitful years, we developed the ministry together, operating in our particular strengths and gifts.

While I was stateside that summer of 1980, I also attended the annual Christian Artists Seminar (CAS) in Estes Park,

Colorado. Cam Floria, director of the acclaimed Continental Singers, created CAS to inspire artists from all disciplines and nations to take up his dream for nurturing creative and spiritual renewal. Cam's vision fit well with mine. I volunteered to be on their steering committee as they prepared to expand the CAS into Western Europe. I continued attending and teaching at CAS events. Through this networking partnership, I met several of my future, most-dedicated MFM musicians: Cathy Carter-Heiser, Fred Dallenbach, and Belinda Van de Loo-Kuhn.

I had hoped our first MMS site would be YWAM Heidebeek, with all its rural charm, but Floyd proposed launching it in Amsterdam, where he was forming a new base. I was glad to be under his leadership, but pioneering in that unique new setting presented many challenges.

YWAM had recently acquired a mouse-infested, derelict building they called the Samaritan's Inn. General William Booth of the Salvation Army preached there in the mid-1800s. The Children of God cult occupied it for a season before abandoning it. It was located across the street from Amsterdam's Central Train Station and adjacent to the Zeedijk—one of the most famous drug streets in Europe.

While it was unoccupied, authorities purposely tore up the inside, filled it with junk, and broke the pipes to discourage *krakers* (squatters). Renovations were still underway when we moved in, so we always had to be careful. The MMS students lived in two rooms, one for guys and one for girls. Only a few toilets worked.

We ate our meals downstairs in a makeshift dining room, along with the entire YWAM Amsterdam family, and shared kitchen duties. A dingy basement room infested with rats and mice served as our practice space.

I slept on a folding couch in a tiny room with a great view of the nightly mouse traffic streaming under my door from the hall. I was losing sleep night after night. So I prayed, *Oh Lord, please heal me of this fear or get rid of these mice.* I felt like he encouraged me to watch them for a while. I did and concluded they were kind of cute, like Mickey Mouse, and not out to harm me. Their population dropped when our construction workers made rubber-band guns and held contests to see who could shoot the most mice.

Nine students attended our first MMS. The program consisted of a month of spiritual training under teachers like Vineyard movement founder John Wimber and Linda McGowan-Panci, who had compiled a widely used, French, praise songbook. The students also rehearsed daily to prepare for six weeks of outreach. Thankfully, most had brought their instruments, and they managed to work in cramped conditions using my small Bose sound system. We taught the students songs in French and German, preparing two small bands headed to France and Germany.

Our staff also stretched to do things they had never done before. Naomi Boshoff's artistic talents were evident to us, so she was assigned to produce publicity materials, such as posters. Meanwhile, her husband, Leon, became a sound tech.

We faced one of our most significant tests of faith as the outreach time neared. The students needed more rehearsals, but Samaritan's Inn pressed us to move out a week early to make room for another outreach team. We located a farmhouse north of Amsterdam where we could stay and rehearse, but we didn't have a way to transport fifteen adults and three children. On the morning of our scheduled departure, we still had no vehicle. "You all pray for transportation," I said to the class, "while I go to the office and see if God provides a contact who can help."

To rent a large van for a week would be pretty expensive. *Maybe God wants to give us the money,* I thought. As I sat praying, Landa Cope, a YWAM teacher based in Switzerland, walked into the office.

"Hi, Karen! What are you doing?" she asked.

"I'm praying for a large van that could take our musicians up north for a week," I answered. Half-joking, I added, "Do you know of one?"

"I think I do know of one," she said. "I have a friend in Switzerland who is Dutch and has a van just sitting at his home here in Holland." Landa called him immediately, and he agreed to let us use the van as long as we paid the insurance when we used it. That was amazing! Not only did we have a great rehearsal week, but the provision of a van heightened our sense of mission as we saw evidence of God at work on our behalf.

Our diligence paid off as some of those first students returned to do a DTS, joined the Musicians for Missions staff, and helped more musicians serve in missions.

Musicians often find it challenging to fit into ministry organizational structures because they need creative opportunities, rehearsal time, sound equipment, concert planning and setup, travel, etc. Musicians for Missions and YWAM Amsterdam gave our musicians an environment to thrive in their gifts and callings. Our ministry home came complete with community, leadership, and accountability structures. Within it, students received solid spiritual and practical oversight. Above all, they had the freedom, time, and space to do their work and grow in ministry.

The leadership of YWAM Amsterdam didn't try to direct our vision. Still, like every other ministry under their covering, we were encouraged to seek the Lord and learn how to conduct our ministry in a purposeful, organized way. Our musicians were required to present concrete goals and budgets. We had to consider what tours and concerts were most important, what equipment we needed most, the frequency of meetings, and who would own the album projects.

As MFM grew and matured, we became a close-knit family of "musicianaries." We saw ourselves as Christ's ambassadors in Holland and other countries.

Amsterdam was a city full of opportunity. When our musicians were home, they could play at YWAM's coffeehouse, help the local church with worship services, or engage street people through evangelism and mercy ministry. One summer, MFM served Floyd's vision for an ambitious week of evangelistic concerts called Rock Week.

During the summer, well-known Christian bands and musicians were often in Holland for the annual Youth for Christ

Flevo Festival or the European Christian Artists Seminar. We took advantage of this opportunity by inviting bands and musicians like Servant, Greg Voltz, Darrell Mansfield, and Resurrection Band to perform at Rock Week. They jumped at the chance to play in Amsterdam for free housing and meals. We also asked Windows, YWAM Hong Kong's dance team, to do open-air performances on Dam Square, just outside our concert venue. They became a calling card, drawing people in with their modern dance.

Phil Keaggy and his wife happened to be visiting Amsterdam during Rock Week and asked if YWAM could provide them a hospitality room for a couple of days. I asked Phil if he would consider playing a few songs to open for a guest band. For a place to stay and an Amsterdam T-shirt, this gracious man and superb guitarist got up on stage and blessed us with his music.

Many people came to the Lord through the concerts, but the week was not without its challenges. One afternoon, we hosted the Maranatha! punk band Undercover. About forty skinheads and punkers pushed toward the elevated dance stage in front of the band as they played. One of the punkers began spitting on the band members, who took it in stride for a while. But when the punker continued, Joey, one of the musicians, threw water on his abuser, who promptly jumped up on the stage. The fight was on!

I was on the balcony watching and praying hard because I didn't know what else to do. Several YWAM leaders finally stepped in to break it up. After the concert, Joey and members of YWAM Amsterdam's Steiger 14 ministry talked to the punkers for hours. Some of those hard-core kids later became part of a church Steiger 14 started.

YWAM Amsterdam also hosted a yearly outreach program called Summer of Service, which trained and sent out traveling teams. They used street dramas to draw crowds and creatively present the gospel. Once I had seen the power and success of this approach, I knew we needed to be involved. The first MMS had been just a music training school that included a time of outreach. But I envisioned us serving alongside Summer of Service and having the same kind of impact. It seemed natural for us to join forces.

In MFM's second year, we shifted our focus and converted the MMS to become Musicians Summer of Service (MSOS). We offered the same training but geared it toward a more evangelism-oriented outreach. Over the next ten years, we recruited and prepared as many as twenty participants a summer for MSOS outreaches, sending bands to multiple countries. These outreaches became the primary source for recruiting MFM staff.

As MFM grew, our staff and musicians followed their particular callings out to the nations. Eddie and Vickie Huff made their way to Germany while Philippe Bogdon went to Switzerland. Dave and Becky Durham joined YWAM Switzerland and became well known in the French-speaking world. Denny and Maureen Hurst moved to Italy to promote concerts, and Leon and Naomi Boshoff returned to South Africa to pioneer a Christian Artists Seminar there. Eike Martins returned to Germany to assist a ministry in Berlin.

Other musicians remained in Amsterdam to engage in its many ministry possibilities. MFM musicians served, taught, and recruited at YWAM Go Festivals or helped Operation

Mobilization with their Love Europe festivals. Some joined other YWAM locations and ministries, like Mercy Ships, to help with projects worldwide. And whenever and wherever the world gathered for the Olympic Games, MFM musicians came together with other YWAMers to share the gospel through music. The vision I'd had while traveling solo as a Maranatha! artist had become a God-reality!

Floyd McClung's leadership was critical to the birth and success of MFM, including my role in it. He made room for MFM among all the YWAM ministries in Holland. He was not controlling, but he applied loving discipline and guidance whenever and wherever necessary. Floyd built the whole ministry on mutual trust. He actively mentored me and others in leadership skills and insisted we hear from God together about upcoming ministry goals.

Each year, he gathered the YWAM Amsterdam staff for At Home Week, a time for all staff to wait on God concerning the upcoming year. One time, I'd been invited to the World Baptist Conference in Prague, Czechoslovakia. I booked the conference, not realizing it fell during At Home Week. I didn't discover my mistake until after the conference coordinators worked months to obtain a special visa. I went to Floyd to let him know.

"I'm sorry, Floyd," I said, "but I won't be able to be at the At Home Week because of an international conference commitment." Then I explained the circumstances to him. He looked at me for a moment.

"You're still on staff here, aren't you?"

"Well, yes."

"Then you *will* be here like all the other staff."

"But this is important," I argued.

"So is At Home Week," he said.

It was tempting to go anyway. But as I prayed, the Lord spoke clearly to me. It was not worth damaging my long-term relationship with my leader by going on a short-term outreach I had mistakenly booked. Floyd did compromise, but he made it clear I needed to be home the first few days of At Home Week. I canceled the first few concerts in Prague, and I was at peace with the decision, even though I was embarrassed about disappointing my Prague sponsors.

Years later, I asked Floyd if he remembered the incident. He did. With characteristic humility, he said, "I wonder if I made the right decision." I was sure I had made the right decision in staying. It affirmed my trust in his leadership and our community.

Floyd and I had another occasion to practice mutual honor and respect when we clashed one time at the close of YWAM Amsterdam's Rock Week festival. We were coming to the end of the nine-day concert series. MFM staff members were responsible for daily equipment setups and teardowns, sound, and transportation for the guest bands. After nine long and stressful days, I was running on empty.

We were scrambling to get the sound check finished for a well-known American band on the last night. We scheduled one of our summer outreach bands to open for them, but because the guest band demanded so much preconcert time for their sound check, there was no time left for the MSOS band to do theirs. I should have strong-armed the visiting band to ensure enough time for the second sound check, but I didn't.

It was getting late, and just before we were to start, our sound man took a quick restroom break. The crowd was getting restless, and Floyd, who was to give the message that night, was nervous.

"If we don't get this going, people are going to leave," he said.

"We'll start soon," I assured him. Then, to my surprise, he went to the front, welcomed the audience, and started the show without my nod.

As soon as the MSOS band launched into their first song, the speakers screamed with feedback. The sound man came running from the restroom when he realized we'd started without him. But even by the second song, the sound was awful.

"Get that group off the stage! The sound is terrible!" Floyd said. I looked up at him.

"I will not take them off the stage! You shouldn't have started the concert; they didn't get a sound check. It's not the band's fault!"

Floyd was still upset but agreed to let them finish. I went and stood in a dark corner and let the tears roll. I felt like beating my head against the wall; I was so tired and upset.

The following week, when the festival was over, we were praying around a table at one of our leadership meetings. I felt a tap on my shoulder. I opened my eyes, and there was Floyd, on his knees, eye level with me.

"God has convicted me," he began. "I was wrong. I shouldn't have taken over the other night; I usurped your authority. Will you forgive me?"

"Yes, I forgive you," I said. I had been hurt and offended, but I was also released as soon as I released Floyd by speaking those important words. Several days later, Floyd stopped me as we passed in a hallway.

"I don't know if I have repented enough about this situation," he said, and I released him by voicing my forgiveness a second time.

Not many people would have come and humbled themselves the way Floyd did, but he always practiced the principles he preached. In those early years in Amsterdam, I learned what it meant to be a leader worth following from a pro. It was this solid and principled-yet-caring style of leadership that saved me when I tumbled deep into sin.

CHAPTER 15

A Great Fall and
Gracious Restoration

"We hope for what we do not see. Washed and waiting.
That is my life—my identity as one who is forgiven
and spiritually cleansed and my struggle
as one who perseveres with a frustrating thorn in the flesh,
looking forward to what God has promised to do."

—Wesley Hill, *Washed and Waiting*

I suffered my greatest moral failure while working under Floyd and Sally's compassionate leadership. Throughout my crisis, the McClungs modeled another critical leadership principle: God doesn't throw us away when we fall. Therefore, as leaders, we shouldn't give up on others who fail.

By 1982, despite my accomplishments as a musician with Maranatha! Music and Musicians for Missions, I still had significant insecurities concerning men. I worked confidently in ministry with most men, but it didn't take much for me to feel intimidated or abandoned. A teasing remark from a man could trigger feelings of rejection in me.

I longed for a soul mate and wanted to build a genuine, caring relationship with a man that could lead to marriage. I struggled to understand why I was not able to develop one. Was it because of past conflicts with my stepfather? Was it because, as a performer and leader, I was somehow intimidating to men? Or was it because my expectations for a relationship were unrealistic? I held onto hope that God would give me revelation and healing. However, I didn't know how to initiate a healthy relationship at that point.

Due to my unresolved insecurities, I looked to women for meaningful relationships. I must confess that I found myself attracted to women as well as men for years. In my search for someone who would care about me as an individual, I fell into an immoral liaison with a woman. This unhealthy attachment began—as so many do—with rationalization.

This woman showed care, concern, and tenderness toward me—the same kind of attention that starts affairs between all emotionally hungry people. It began with notes of encouragement and acts of thoughtfulness, the very things I longed for from men but never seemed to receive. Once I tasted what I perceived as genuine love, our relationship became physical, and I started to tell myself little lies: *I'm different. I deserve this. God will understand.* Soon our relationship spiraled into an avalanche of lies and secrecy.

I knew of Christian leaders who had fallen away from God and lost relationships because of moral failures. And here I was, falling into the same kind of self-deception and concealment. Sadly, I had been down this road before, once in college and during my time at Calvary Chapel. While I found healing to some degree, I didn't realize how deep the roots of rejection and abuse went inside me.

When I stumbled this time, I recognized it as a *pattern*, and I knew I had to break the secrets and lies and move toward counseling.

My love for God was too precious to slap him in the face by continuing in that immoral lifestyle. He had shown me the richness of his love, blessings, and grace—even giving me the song "Seek Ye First" and establishing me in ministry. How could I dishonor him after all he had done for me? How could I open the door for unbelievers to scoff and say: *See? Those Christians are just a bunch of hypocrites; they say one thing and do another.*

Years earlier, while at Calvary Chapel, I confessed to Pastor Chuck. He reminded me that *God could forgive any sin* brought into the light. But we must be willing to repent (before someone we trust) and turn away from our sin. Breaking old patterns only happens when we get at the roots of the thinking that led us there in the first place.

When it came out in a conversation between Floyd and me that I was in an unrighteous relationship, he and Sally did not turn me away from missions and ministry. Instead, they gathered me into their wise and loving counsel and, with tenderness, walked with me toward healing and restoration.

I opened up to the McClungs and poured out the whole story of my daddy's death and how I had felt abandoned and left alone, without a father to take care of me. I revealed the sexual abuses stretching back to my childhood. That I had been groped, sexually used, and abandoned emotionally and relationally, even by men I loved and trusted. I shared how it seemed as if the men attracted to me only saw me as a sex object, not someone they wanted to love and protect. As I confided these things to the McClungs, they embraced me and wept alongside me.

I was struck by how intently Floyd listened and how freely he cried for me and with me. Here was an earnest man who felt the injustice of what had happened to me, and he cared! Here was a strong man who did not reject me or hide his feelings from me but reached out with compassion! I had experienced heartache at the hands of some immature and selfish men, but God showed me through Floyd's fatherly example a reflection of his own heart. Floyd and Sally wisely initiated a soul-searching time for me that set me on the path toward restoration and wholeness.

Christian leaders sometimes deal with fallen brothers and sisters by sending them home. I'm so grateful that the YWAM leaders I've worked with are more concerned about restoration than perfection in ministry. I had sinned, and I was working to break sin's hold on my life. But because my YWAM family surrounded me with mercy instead of judgment, I was not disqualified from fellowship or ministry.

My leaders at YWAM Amsterdam committed to seeking the Lord with me about God's plan for my healing. At Floyd's request, I handed the MFM reins to Eddie and other staff. I remained on staff but stepped out of public ministry for a season. Floyd challenged me to use this time to let God deal deeply in my heart. He said, "If you are willing to do that, nothing can hold you back from the ministry God has given you."

Floyd and Sally began meeting with me regularly to help me walk through the process. When my sin came into the light, I'd been preparing to leave for the most extensive tour of the United States and Canada I had ever done. My mom had gone to great pains to book it for me. As always, rather than telling me what to do, Floyd urged me to hear from God for myself about what I should do.

I prayed and sensed I needed to cancel the tour. When I called and told my mom, she was disappointed. "Can't you just repent and go on?"

"I have repented, but I can't minister to others in this condition. Sometimes you have to stop and get down to the root of things."

Mom understood, and we canceled the tour. I was blessed when several concert sponsors responded, saying, "Tell Karen we are praying for her. Tell her to contact us when she is ready."

My YWAM Amsterdam family knew I had a tour booked, so telling them I was not going was the next step. I explained it in a way that made it sound like I was merely taking time to press into God. Once again, Floyd questioned me, "Were you being honest? What do you need to tell our Amsterdam family about your tour?"

A week later, at the next staff meeting, I got up again, my knees and voice shaking with emotion. "I have not been in a good place. I've fallen into sin, so I need to spend time with the Lord, to repent and get counsel." That was an enormous step for me, even though I didn't give details. The point of my public confession was not to humiliate me but to let my family know I was in a tender place and needed their prayers and compassion. And that's what they gave me.

When King David faced his sin, he wrote, "The sacrifice you desire is a broken spirit. You will not reject a broken and repentant heart, O God" (Psalm 51:17 NLT).

We've all sinned, and we all need to walk in the light and fellowship. Living in secrecy regarding my unhealthy relationship had been a sure road to trouble. For the next eight months, I was out of public ministry. I served at the YWAM base, prayed, fasted, received counsel, read books, and rested in the love and prayers of my YWAM Amsterdam family.

By current society standards, some might think I was trying to change what culture now perceives as a perfectly "natural" way people are born—gay. I spent many hours turning this over in my mind. But I believe God's Word remains clear and firm about our sexual identity. I've always based my beliefs and hope on that. For that reason, I was determined to follow him at all costs.

I was offered an apartment at an old Dutch estate in the forest for a five-day personal retreat. Those days were intense, and at one point, I grew so angry I jumped in my car and drove to Heidebeek to talk with my former DTS small group leader. Red-faced from crying and complaining to God, I said to Ron,

"Why is God punishing me?"

"God's discipline is not punishment," he said in his compassionate way. "He disciplines those he loves. It's training for the future."

Discipline, not punishment. Training for the future. These were revelations to me. I drove slowly back to my retreat house as the overcast skies began to scatter snowflakes. Back at the apartment, I drew the drapes back and looked out at the second-story view for hours. I watched as God painted the green-gray forest in pure white. Then Isaiah 1:18 came to my mind: "'Come now, and let us reason together,' says the LORD, 'though your sins are like scarlet, they shall be as white as snow'" (NKJV).

As this truth filled my heart, I responded by writing a simple song:

> I stand in the righteousness of Jesus the Son,
> For my own ways falter, and broken I've become.
> I want to walk in his Spirit, moved by his love,
> And trust my Father to change me to be like his Son.

CHAPTER 16

God in the Urban War Zone

In the eye of the storm, you remain in control.
In the middle of the war, you guard my soul.

"In the Eye of the Storm" by Bryan Fowler and Ryan Dale Stevenson
© Capitol Christian Music Group

Amsterdam is a city known worldwide for its open prostitution and drug use. Those peddling these vices try to make it seem glamorous and enticing. The Lord brought me face-to-face with the dark underbelly of this world during my time away from music ministry.

Many of my YWAM coworkers engaged in outreach into Amsterdam's notorious Red Light District, which Floyd renamed the Promised Land. One was a South African woman named Marietha, who daily escorted the children of our Samaritan's Inn families to a Catholic school located in the Promised Land.

One day, Marietha ran into Natasha, one of the children she knew from the Catholic School. A muscular, six-foot Indonesian man accompanied her. Natasha seemed excited to see Marietha and began pleading with her.

"My mommy's very sick. Can you help her?" Natasha's mother, Ilsa, was a prostitute. Marietha had met her at the school once. Marietha looked at the man with Natasha.

"What do you know about this? Who are you?"

He evaded her eyes. "I'm Robby, Ilsa's boyfriend. Yes, she's very sick. She's home with Natasha's brother, Vincent. We came out to get some food."

Marietha's missionary heart kicked in. "May I go home with you and see if I can help?"

Robby shifted uncomfortably. "Sure," he said. It's not far from here." He nodded in the direction they needed to go.

Marietha followed the pair through the Red Light District to a housing complex. She climbed the stairs to a dingy apartment. Someone had shattered the glass in the door, and the front room reeked of tobacco smoke, urine, and vomit. Natasha's two-year-old brother was running loose on the trash-strewn floor. Her mother, Ilsa, a twenty-two-year-old woman, lay on a dirty mattress on the floor, deathly ill from a dose of bad heroin.

Marietha looked at Robby. It was clear he was Ilsa's pimp, not her boyfriend, as he had led Marietha to believe. She took charge. "We need to get her to the hospital. I will care for the children while she is there."

Robby grunted his approval, appearing glad to be freed from this "problem."

Marietha called a taxi and managed to get Ilsa to the hospital. Then she took the children to her place.

When we learned of this situation, our whole YWAM family began praying for Ilsa and her children. Marietha regularly visited her in the hospital, and Ilsa soon accepted the Lord.

Once Ilsa got out of the hospital, we looked for ways to keep her out of prostitution. She began volunteering in our YWAM community. We set her up in a new apartment with a young Dutch woman named Herma. But Ilsa's headstrong personality and loose child-rearing drove Herma away. Ilsa also had asked Robby to come and stay, still reliant on the man guilty of abusing her.

We all wanted to see Ilsa in a safe place and growing in her new faith. I got the idea that I should live with her and the kids. I prayed about it and proposed it to our leaders, who surprised me by giving me their blessing. At first, I wondered what I was thinking. I had been quite content sharing a nice room with two other Christian women. Ilsa lived in a rough, dangerous area. I was also a bit insecure about life with two small children. But I chose to view it as a new adventure and prayed the Lord would use me there.

Ilsa and I worked together, cleaning around the YWAM community. As I became part of their family at home, Natasha would come to my room every morning, get up on my bed, and talk to me in Dutch. My music ministry consisted of putting the kids to bed with songs and prayers each night for the next couple of months. After that, I would play my guitar, and Ilsa and I would sing worship songs together. These worship times caused Ilsa to open up about her life struggles. As with most women who had been in prostitution, rejection, violence, and sexual abuse scarred her early life. She still had lots of pain bottled up inside her.

At one point, Ilsa's kids got the measles, and she received instructions to quarantine them at home and not expose others. Jon Peterson, one of our YWAM leaders, made the decision, and I was with Ilsa and the kids when he broke the news to them. She exploded. *Nobody was going to tell her what to do!* She doubled up her fists and probably would have punched Jon if a parade of guests visiting the ministry hadn't come into the room at that awkward moment.

Ilsa grabbed her kids and bolted out the door, declaring she was going to "kill Herma." She still blamed her ex-roommate for any problems she had in our YWAM community. I ran ahead to warn Herma while my friend Naomi chased Ilsa down the street to calm her. Ilsa finally broke down and cried, accepting the quarantine and somehow surviving it.

Our apartment was in a ten-story high-rise in a crime-ridden area where someone had robbed some YWAMers at knifepoint once. One morning after worship, Christine, my prophetic friend from New Zealand, handed me a piece of paper. "This is for you from the Lord," she said. It read: "A thousand may fall at your side, ten thousand at your right hand, but it will not come near you" (Psalm 91:7 NIV). I thanked her and put it in my pocket, wondering what it meant.

After Ilsa and the kids and I had gone to bed that night, I awoke to loud banging on the apartment door. I threw on my robe and ran out to see what was going on. There stood Robby—drunk and belligerent.

"Ilsa is my woman, and I am staying right here!"

Just then, tiny Ilsa appeared. "No, you are not!"

As Robby lunged for her, Ilsa punched him in the face. "Get out!"

Robby growled and hit her back. The two started pushing and shoving, their voices rising in a barrage of threats and curses in Dutch.

"Ilsa! What's going on?" I kept asking, trying without success to keep the peace.

When Robby slammed his fist into the door, punching a hole all the way through, I began to get scared. Ilsa already had bruises on her arm from where he had grabbed her. She was more angry than afraid, but I was scared for her—and us.

Then I remembered the Scripture verse Christine had given me that morning, and it dawned on me—God knew this was going to happen and had sent me a promise of his protection! With new courage, I took Ilsa aside.

"Ilsa," I said, "as long as Robby is here, I can't stay."

"Well, I don't want him here, but I don't think he'll leave."

"Do you want to go with me?"

"Yes!" she said, and while she went to get the kids ready to go, I began reasoning with Robby.

"Robby, Ilsa and I have to take the kids and leave."

"That's ridiculous! Why would you leave?"

"Because you are here," I said. As we talked, Robby shifted between anger and hurt, saying things like: "Nobody likes me. People want to take my wife and children away from me. You don't care about me." Even though Ilsa was not his wife, he did have an attachment to her.

"But we *do* care about you, and so does God! We've been praying for you, Robby." He broke down sobbing, and I could hear the hurt in his voice, even though he was still volatile.

"We have to go now," I told him. "But if you're going to stay, call out to God. Ask him to show you if he is real. And I promise you that I will pray for you all night."

Ilsa and I bundled ourselves and the kids up to face the cold winter's night outside. We made our way to another YWAM apartment in a neighboring building. I kept my fear in check by remembering the Scripture Christine had given me. As soon as I got Ilsa and the kids situated, I made a pot of coffee and kept my promise to stay up and pray for Robby all night. He had chosen to stay after we left, and he tore the place up. The neighbors called the police, but they didn't do anything because nobody was getting hurt.

The next day, Ilsa and I didn't go back to the apartment but went to do our regular work at Samaritan's Inn instead. Robby showed up there with my boom box in hand and asked for me. "This is yours," he said. Jon and another YWAM leader sat him down and talked with him. Leaving Ilsa at Samaritan's Inn, some of us went to check the apartment. Robby had ripped up the furniture and beds, broken dishes, and thrown ketchup over everything. But he hadn't touched my stuff, not even my Martin guitar!

Ilsa never returned to that apartment. It seemed better for her to get away from Amsterdam, so we moved her to a Christian community in a Dutch village. As far as I know, she is married today, living in Belgium, and walking with the Lord.

As for me, I still recall the significance of those events. God put his hand on me and encouraged me by sending Christine with a specific word, letting me know that he would protect me as my Father.

CHAPTER 17

Waiting for the Promise

"God's delays are not necessarily God's denials."

—Joy Dawson

T ouring and performing on stage had been my life for many years. While I knew this break was necessary for my spiritual development, I longed to get back into public ministry. When it seemed the time had come, I went to Floyd to let him know I was ready.

"How do you know?" he asked. "How are you getting your direction from God? How has he spoken to you?"

"I don't have a specific word from God, but I am feeling stronger in my faith. I've also gained an understanding of the relational and identity issues that I'd struggled with before."

"Well," he said, "let's go back to God and ask him for confirmation. You need to be sure you heard from him."

Floyd hadn't said no, but he pointed me back to God for a clear word. He was right. I knew I should not be so casual in my approach. When making a big decision, it's vital to seek God for specifics. Throughout the Scriptures, faithful men and women sought God's guidance for everything from battle strategies to travel plans to family matters.

I was disappointed in myself; after all of the teaching and discipleship I'd had, I should have known better than to proceed without clear direction. But I was a doer, ready to get busy again, and it was hard to wait. My desire overrode the more critical need to seek God. That's what had gotten me into trouble in the first place, and no doubt it's the story of why many spiritual leaders have fallen into sin.

I had hoped Floyd would accept my timetable, but being a true discipler, he asked the hard questions. It was humbling. I could see I had lost the fear of God, allowing the temptation to rush ahead of the Lord to blind me. Floyd didn't criticize. He gently urged me to seek God with all my heart and let him be my counselor.

I went back to seeking the Lord for a definitive word, and when I did, he directed me to read the book of Acts. As I read, a phrase jumped out at me, though I had read it a hundred times before: *Wait for the promise of the Father.* I knew God had called me and given me the promise of ministry, but here I was, going through an indefinite period of change and healing. Then it hit me: I still had a call on my life—his promise to me—but he wanted me to wait for him to finish the work he needed to do in me. It was not a matter of if but when!

I told Floyd God wanted me to continue waiting. But what would the Lord have me do while I waited? What did the disciples do while they waited? They prayed, broke bread, fellowshipped, and worshiped together—the very things I was doing with my YWAM Amsterdam family. I continued serving in practical ways.

At one point, Floyd asked me to put together a praise band for our YWAM community. Of course, I said yes. Staying in fellowship with God and his people was the most profound thing I could have done at that time in my life.

A few months later, we gathered at Heidebeek for a national staff conference. During worship at one of the meetings, I noticed some leaders talking among themselves. Soon, Floyd stood up and announced there were people in our midst in need of special prayer. He called out four or five individuals, and I was one of them.

As they surrounded us and sought the Lord in prayer, prophecies began to flow. When they prayed for me, a word came forth saying God was pleased that I had spent this time drawing close to him, and now he was releasing me back into public ministry. As the leaders encouraged me to go out again, Romans 11:29 came to mind. It says: "The gifts and the calling of God are irrevocable" (NASB). I also remembered how Paul and Barnabas received their call during a time of worship in Acts 13. It was a fitting way to reenter ministry.

How to return to ministry was the question. After canceling my tour, I had remained out of ministry and out of touch with my contacts for eight months. As I looked over my calendar, I discovered I had been booked a year in advance for a festival in Germany that I'd forgotten. When I called to inquire about it, they assured me they still expected me. I was right on schedule with God's timing! This festival was part of a recognized European celebration of Pentecost.

It struck me how God was unfolding his plan for me in a significant way. He spoke to me from the book of Acts, where the disciples *waited for the promise of the Father*. Pentecost fulfilled that promise. Now, a Pentecost celebration would fulfill God's promise to *me* of restored life and ministry! The Lord works in beautiful ways! At Floyd's request, I had sought the Lord in detail about what to do, and as a result, I got a specific answer from God. He made sure I didn't miss this powerful connection.

God wants us to meet with him. *He genuinely wants to talk to us.* When God speaks, we may not see the whole picture initially. But he will always give us an accurate road map and timetable to reach our destination.

CHAPTER 18

When It Rains

"Preach the word of God. Be prepared,
whether the time is favorable or not."

—2 Timothy 4:2 (NLT)

My early training and experience with Maranatha! Music taught me to be prayerful, spiritually alert, and respectful in approaching concert audiences. How thankful I was to have learned that lesson as new doors opened for me in Europe!

In 2 Corinthians 6:3–4, Paul says to give "no cause for offense in anything, so that the ministry will not be discredited, but in everything commending ourselves as servants of God" (NASB 1995). I wanted to glorify God in all our efforts. I soon faced situations that could have exposed him and our ministry to misunderstanding and ridicule. I needed his guidance more than ever in times like those.

After Paul instructs us not to give cause for offense and to have the attitude of a servant, he says we may have to serve "by glory and dishonor, by evil report and good report; *regarded* as deceivers and yet true" (v. 8 NASB). On the one hand, people might come up after a concert to tell me they loved the songs; that was the glory. On the other hand, others might come and criticize me for wearing slacks instead of a dress. One time a man said to me, "Who do you think you are ministering the Word? You're a woman." The key was not to feel condemned but to make every effort to prepare and honor the Lord in ways culturally familiar to the people to whom we ministered.

I shared once at a Brethren church in England where women customarily wore a head covering. I hadn't brought one, so they gave me a small scarf to pin over my short hair. As I sang, I realized that my guitar strap had snagged the scarf, slowly pulling it off. I was helpless to do anything about it. By the time I finished the song, the scarf was hanging from the strap. The women's expressions on the front row turned from smiles to worried frowns as they watched this unfold. I was embarrassed, but I couldn't help smiling when I saw YWAMers on the back row giggling. Those sweet Brethren ladies came up afterward and said politely, in their soft British accents, "Oh my, don't worry dear. Thank you for trying."

I taught Musicians for Missions participants to be sensitive and flexible in concert settings. We prayed for God's wisdom as to how to communicate culturally and generationally. We needed to adapt our music, appearance, and approach to the setting while holding fast to God's truth. We asked God to help us prepare for anything that might happen, and we surely needed his help!

On one occasion, I led a Musicians Summer of Service band in Belgium that included a few young women. As I scanned the crowd gathered at the park where we were playing, I noticed a group of four men standing by a tree. They were smoking, talking, and laughing, and I sensed they were up to something. Soon, the men marched up in a line, grabbing at their belts. They halted right in front of us with their hands folded in front of them. I turned to the band as they approached.

"Ladies," I said, "if these guys do anything weird, don't give them the pleasure of your eyes. Look over their heads or anywhere else, but not at them." The four men suddenly dropped their pants, but the band paid no attention. They kept on singing as the concert sponsors ushered the men out.

Sometimes circumstances we saw as problems became open doors for God to move in profound ways. One time, we arranged for a visiting band to play on Dam Square in the heart of Amsterdam. As soon as we set up the sound equipment, it began to rain. The rain forced us to cover everything and seek God about what to do. The visiting band went back to the YWAM base, but many of us stayed. I'm so glad we did because God had a different plan than ours that day.

The rain eased, and we put together a small acoustic band. Floyd got up during our impromptu concert, picked up his little daughter Misha, and began talking about the father heart of God. He explained how Father God wants the right things for his children just as parents want the right things for theirs. One woman in the small audience along with her little boy stood watching, and I later went to talk to her. She was a single mom named Aukje.

"We came downtown to see the movie *Dumbo*," she said, "but the show was sold out. So we came to the Dam, and you were here. I know I have much to learn. I want to do right by my son, but I don't know how."

"I believe God loves your heart attitude about raising your son, and he'll help you if you open your heart to him," I explained.

Aukje wanted to continue talking about God, so I invited her to the coffee bar at Samaritan's Inn. She came several times after that, often bringing friends with her. One night I sensed Aukje was ready to make changes in her life. I explained that she needed to be in a relationship with the Lord to make the right choices. *Was she prepared to receive him?* She was. Aukje went on to take a Discipleship Training School and later became involved in ministry in Cyprus and Israel.

On the day of the concert on the Dam, our big plan had gone awry, but God made way for a willing woman as we waited for his plan. Aukje and I remained friends. I bought a Dumbo stuffed toy and gave it to her with a card that read: *Here's something to remind you of the day you came to Amsterdam to see* Dumbo *and met Jesus instead.*

One of the greatest challenges in ministry is taking a stand for truth in a compromising situation. I received an invitation to play at a coffee bar in a village near Amsterdam. When the sponsors booked me, they said I might remember them from a previous ministry at another church. They gave me the impression they were starting a new fellowship and had the blessing of their former church. It was quite the contrary. This group had split off from the other church due to a significant doctrinal dispute.

When I arrived, they informed me it was not necessary to talk about how to receive Jesus. That was my first red flag. My Grandma Stout had just died, and I had planned to talk about not having any doubts about where she was because she had decided to follow Christ.

After I finished playing, one of the sponsors presented me with a book "to help you understand the Bible." He said to me, "Sister, you don't have to respond right now. Just think about it." I soon discovered my sponsors were Universalists, who believe that all fallen angels, devils, and even Satan himself will be redeemed. For that reason, they say it is not necessary to be saved, only to study the Bible and other books.

Heart pounding, I said to him: "Sir, I don't have to go home and think about it. That is straight from the pit of hell, and I can see now that you brought me here under pretense, making me think you were a branch of the other church. Some people have come specifically to hear me, and you are trying to suck them into your cult. No sir! I'm leaving and will take as many with me as will come." I called for the audience's attention through my Dutch interpreter.

"I know the concert is over, but I have something important I need to share with you," I began. "This group brought me here under pretense. I want you to know I think they teach unbiblical things against Christ's teachings, and they used me to get some of you here. I don't appreciate their tactics. I'm leaving now and won't come back. I would encourage you to do the same!"

I left, shaking and crying. I never had to do anything like that before, but I was grateful that God had given me the courage to stand against these people and their teachings. When the group called me later to get me to reconsider, I gave them a firm no. I can overlook some things I disagree with doctrinally. But I can't and won't go against God's truth that the saving grace of Jesus Christ is the only thing that stands between us and hell.

CHAPTER 19

Opening Hearts and Minds

"For I am about to do something new.
See, I have already begun!"

—Isaiah 43:19 (NLT)

The year 1989 was a milestone, both for Eastern Europe and Youth With A Mission. The collapse of the Soviet Union's "Iron Curtain" opened the way for us to minister in countries where Christian bands like ours had never been before.

I taught and performed at a Christian Artists Seminar in Hungary, where I met Romanian sisters Ana and Rebecca Corlan. "Karen, you must bring this music to Romania. We'll help you do it." And they did! With assistance from their large family and church connections, we launched seminars and concert tours across Romania. It was gratifying to train young worship bands using facilities formerly utilized to indoctrinate youth in communism.

As our contact list grew, we incorporated Romanian nationals into our bands and translated song lyrics to enable audience participation whenever possible. Most of the churches were traditional Romanian Protestant. They feared the Western influence flooding across their borders. Our challenge was to embrace and respect them while helping them grow in the new things God was bringing their way.

We adopted the thinking of Bill Bright, founder of Campus Crusade. He said, "Hold fast to what doesn't change—that's Jesus Christ and the Word of God. But flow with what does change." God's truth never changes, but hairstyles, dress, and music styles will always differ from culture to culture and generation to generation. Building on this foundational and reasonable teaching, we set about helping congregations see the need to reach out to youth in ways that would speak to them without compromising the truth. We went to great lengths to make our music exciting to young people yet acceptable to the older generation.

One Sunday, a pastor approached me and said, "Tonight, you should probably do your concert without drums." One of the church elders had seen us bring in drums (which we used more orchestrally than rock style) and was adamant that we could *not* use them. He believed they were irreverent and of the devil.

"Pastor," I responded, "You have heard our music. What do *you* think of it?"

"Oh, I think it's beautiful."

"Thank you. We want to honor God in all we do. The devil has taken over so much music today, taking our youth along with it. We are working to take those things back."

"I think that is good."

"It is good, but many older people in congregations like yours need to learn this. Pastor, it is your responsibility to teach them."

He agreed reluctantly but said, "I would like you to explain all this to them first."

So I began the service by laying the truth out before a people who did love God and wanted to do things biblically. I read these words from verses 3–6 of Psalm 150:

> Praise him with the sounding of the trumpet,
> praise him with the harp and lyre,
> praise him with timbrel and dancing,
> praise him with the strings and pipe,
> praise him with the clash of cymbals. . . .
> Let everything that has breath praise the LORD. (NIV)

"Tonight," I said, "we want to present to you some wonderful truths from the Bible. We've had our music translated so you can understand it, and we're so glad your wonderful choir will sing it for us. I know that using drums in your sanctuary may seem irreverent to many of you. Some instruments, such as the electric guitar and the drums, have been used for evil purposes. But tonight, we're going to take them back from Satan and use them for God's glory. Let's pray and commit this music to the Lord!"

The congregation loved it—little old ladies came to shake our hands afterward, wishing us *pace* (pronounced "pa-chay"), which means "peace." These folks understood the language, Bible verses, and music we had used because we walked them into a new experience one step at a time.

One of my favorite strategies for pushing through cultural barriers and leading folks into a full expression of worship began through a YWAM production dubbed *Konsert voor de Koning*

(Concert for the King). The program followed up YWAM Holland's Dutch praise recordings *Muzik voor de Koning* (Music for the King).

The Dutch Reformed Church was skeptical of new forms of praise music. Their worship consisted of hymns from the traditional Johan de Heer hymnal. Our goal was to find creative ways to blend old worship expressions with the new songs on the Dutch praise recordings so the whole body of Christ in Holland could grow together in worship.

We knew folks would more likely attend at a familiar setting, so we reserved large Dutch Reformed churches for the tour. Rather than calling the event a praise and worship evening, we approached it more as a concert. We made it colorful and unique by combining dance, lights, a choir, a praise band (including orchestral instruments), and formal touches such as responsive readings and a display of the altar's communion elements.

The program began with a lone violin. A dozen choir members entered, carrying lighted candles and singing in Dutch, "We have gathered here in Jesus' name to worship you, O Holy One." Once they placed the candles on the communion table, our narrators, Peter Helms and Jeff Fountain, announced that "all those gathered would be bringing an offering of worship to the King." By helping them see that they were participants, not spectators, we opened the way to introduce our traditional audience to more contemporary worship expressions.

Peter and Jeff gave sermonettes on praise and worship throughout the evening, using the Bible to lay a foundation for leading people into participation. We introduced dance using

Jewish music and choreography, showing how Miriam led the Israelite women to sing, dance, and play tambourines to celebrate the Red Sea crossing and the destruction of the Pharaoh's army. And we used drama to visually present the story of God sending his Son to be crucified for our sins.

As the concert progressed, we led people in new songs, giving them opportunities to try new worship methods, including clapping and raising their hands to the Lord. A friend of mine overheard two older Dutch Reformed women discussing whether they should raise their hands. Jeff had just given the scriptural basis for it from Psalm 63:3–4, which reads: "Because thy lovingkindness is better than life, my lips shall praise thee. Thus will I bless thee while I live: I will lift up my hands in thy name" (KJV). One of the women commented, "Well, it *is* biblical." Later, my friend saw both lift their hands in praise. Beautiful!

Each concert ended on a traditional note with the hymn "*U Zij de Glorie*" ("Yours Is the Glory"). It's a triumphant song Dutch Reformed congregations sing at the end of many events. The response to the program as a whole was so positive that people often told us, "We didn't want it to end!"

We toured Holland presenting different versions of Concert for the King for three years. Our audiences easily entered into worship because we used elements they could understand. It blessed us to see hearts and minds open up to new ways of expressing adoration to God. As our Dutch brothers and sisters grew in their understanding, these new elements were no longer threatening. We saw the lasting fruit of our efforts as Christian dance groups and contemporary bands began popping up around the country.

Willingness to engage cultures and generations through preparedness, gentle instruction, and sensitivity enables people to meet God in fresh ways. It's a template for growth that continues to bring together believers in Christ around the world.

CHAPTER 20

The South Africa Years

Every tribe and nation, people and language,
All who've heard and answered the call,
Bringing forth their worship before the Father;
Every voice enhancing the song.

—"Every Tribe and Nation" by David and Rebecca Durham © 2003 Did You Look Music/ASCAP
as recorded on Karen Lafferty's *Multitudes—The Sound of Many Nations*, © Heart Cry Music

In the 1980s, *apartheid*—Afrikaans for "apartness"—was the law of the land in South Africa. Blacks and coloreds (those of mixed racial and cultural heritage) were segregated from South African whites. Discrimination, violence, and fear filled their everyday lives. But a global tide of resistance to this evil was rising, inspired by the courage of activists like Nelson Mandela and Stephen Biko.

I believed artists should play a role in helping end apartheid. Secular entertainers showed their opposition by boycotting Sun City, a luxury gambling resort that attracted the country's rich and famous. Fifty secular artists did a collaborative recording called "I Ain't Gonna Play Sun City." The song became the rallying cry for those opposed to apartheid. Many Christian artists also boycotted South Africa, but I believed God wouldn't boycott— he would engage. He would have us take his call to repentance and redemption wherever people needed it.

YWAM was pioneering ministries across South Africa. My association with Leon and Naomi Boshoff and their son Timothy opened the door to my involvement. The Boshoffs had returned home to South Africa in 1983 with a vision for training Christian musicians. They wanted to help all musicians—black, colored, or white—combat apartheid by living out Christian principles. The Boshoffs had attended our Christian Artists Seminars in Holland, and in 1984, they founded Christian Artists South Africa (CASA). Under this banner, they organized the first South African training seminar, held in December 1985.

I worked with Leon and Naomi on some aspects of the event. The Boshoffs organized CASA to represent the whole of South Africa as well as other countries. Invitations went out to artists of all races. The nature and structure of the seminar provided a platform for real change. In this safe environment, we could gather as Christians and musicians. We could listen to and learn from one another, mutually discovering ways to bring change to South Africa using the arts to benefit all. Although not political in purpose, the seminar still provided a place where people could openly discuss injustice issues and come before the Lord to resolve long-standing racial tensions.

The logistics of that first CASA, located at the Youth for Christ retreat center in Magaliesburg, were challenging. One of the most pressing issues for the Boshoffs and their staff was transporting large black choirs from the townships to the seminar site and dealing with logistics such as food, housing, hospitality, and stage management. Because our spirit of unity was strong, we worked through problems with minimal tension. Many organizations, churches, and individuals stood with us, praying for us and working hard to help effect change.

The seminar drew eight hundred participants. We showed equal respect and favor to artists from all walks of life, regardless of race, color, or creed. It was the first time many of them had eaten together, much less shared a room with someone of a different race. We believed face-to-face communication was integral to bringing down barriers associated with apartheid. This Christian artist gathering was the perfect place to start. As unusual as the CASA arrangement was, we encountered little resistance.

Inspiring messages from speakers and musicians filled our days, focusing on unity in Jesus. Our nights consisted of concerts featuring international artists from the USA and Europe. They included, among others, Scott Wesley Brown, Bobby Jones and the New Life Singers, Bobby Michaels, and myself playing alongside black choirs from the townships and local artists like Victor Phume and the Syndicates (a black South African group of musicians), Liz Pass (a white South African), Katie Pennington (an American living in South Africa), and Trevor Sampson (a colored musician from Capetown). Friends First, with bandmates Malcolm du Plessis, Nick Paton, and Steve McEwen, played a significant role. The Holy Spirit moved the band members to connect with their black brothers and sisters. Black musicians at CASA were astonished to hear three white guys playing African-style music.

Malcolm later recalled how one of the most influential Christian songs to come out of the apartheid era was written one night at that first seminar:

> About midnight, there were about ten of us sitting in a room at this conference centre. There were five white guys and five black guys all talking, and the one guy, Victor Mangani, said, "Hey, we feel so much closer to you white guys." Then, Danny Bridges grabbed his guitar, played a G chord, and sang, "We feel so much closer." Within minutes, four different guys contributed lyrically, and the song *"Masihlanganeni"* (Zulu for "We Feel So Much Closer") was written.

Friends First and Victor Phume and the Syndicates performed the new song at a joint session the next day. Lingering over the words "we feel so much closer," these multiracial musicians ushered in a glorious time of worship, resulting in prayer for forgiveness and reconciliation and ending in a glorious celebration. As the seminar ended that night, I knew it had been well worth the toil, time, and money we had poured into it. It was the first of several artist gatherings where we learned, worshiped, and shared all together in a spirit of unity. It was a spirit opposite from apartheid.

There was always an element of risk involved with ministry in South Africa. One time, Naomi and I drove by ourselves to a gathering at a nearby township. Naomi took a wrong exit on our way back, and we ended up in an unknown township. In most of the black communities, racial tensions ran high. They would likely perceive two strange white women in a BMW as "rich whites" associated with apartheid. Worse yet, there was a demonstration going on down the street. About two hundred people were jumping up and down and waving flags. If the mob had turned its attention toward us, we would have been in serious trouble. We hightailed it out of there as fast as we could. Though we worked for peace, we could never take the lingering hostility lightly in South Africa.

On another occasion, Scott Wesley Brown, Bob Fitts, Bobby Michaels, the Boshoffs, I, and others gathered for an evening *braai,* a South African cookout. We met at the home of a couple helping with an upcoming Christian Artists Seminar. It was a quiet country setting, and we were in the backyard, sitting on blankets and singing. I was playing the song "I Have You in My Heart." Just as I was about to sing, "Press on, my friends, to know Him / For to live is Christ and we die to win," I heard a bang, and a bullet whizzed over my head.

A bolt of fear ran through me as we all scrambled to get out of the light. *Why was somebody trying to kill us?* I had never felt fear like this in Amsterdam's red-light district, where men could easily accost a woman. Hiding behind the electric piano, it startled me to think my life could be in danger from people who didn't want us in South Africa.

The guys began crawling through the grass in the dark to see if they could locate the shooter. Leon got on the mic and said, "Whoever is doing that, stop it!" Then Bob got up and went, alone, to the mic. He began singing and leading us in spiritual warfare, and I realized I let him take the risk while I sat in the dark, afraid.

I can't let him die alone, I thought. Sheepishly, I got up and joined him. By God's grace, that evening was not our time to die.

I lay awake that night, pondering questions God had placed on my heart before. *Would I be willing to die for Christ, to go anywhere, even into dangerous areas?* I had a restless, sobering time of soul-searching before sleep finally came.

Apartheid ended in 1990. Several years later, Naomi began working with a Christian South African vocal group called Impulse. I was impressed with their precision and standard of excellence. Together, we brought the group to the US in 1994 for a tour extending from Miami, Florida, to Tucson, Arizona.

Impulse had so much to give, and Americans were delighted to meet genuine Africans. When the group arrived at the Miami airport, some black airport stewards asked where they were from. When they discovered Impulse was a South African choir, they asked them to sing. Impulse sang a cappella on the spot, and it was *big* singing— from the high "mamas" to the low basses—attracting a large crowd.

Though Impulse was a Christian choir, I was able to get them into five public schools in Santa Fe, New Mexico. People welcomed them simply because they were from another culture. Another fantastic connection happened because their visit was during the first year black South Africans could vote. A few months earlier, Amy Biehl, a young woman from Santa Fe, had gone to South Africa to help black people learn about the voting process. Tragically, she was attacked by a mob and stabbed to death while escorting home one of her African friends. Amy's family and friends had put together a walkathon to raise money for a scholarship in her name. They asked Impulse to perform at a high school assembly and to promote the event. After performing several songs for a wildly enthusiastic audience, Impulse leader Peter Thafeni addressed the students.

"When we got here today," he said, "they told us about the murder of Amy Biehl, who had come to South Africa to help our people. We are so sorry to hear of this, and we want to ask you to forgive us. We have suffered much injustice and death ourselves because of apartheid. But we are Christians and have learned we need to forgive people who hurt us because Jesus Christ forgave us. It doesn't help to be angry and bitter."

Impulse's concert in Tucson was scheduled during a Sunday morning church service. Unexpectedly, TV camerapeople showed up for the service. The visiting choir drew attention because this was the first day South African blacks could cast votes. When asked what they thought of their country's historic election, the singers replied: "We want to work together for a better South Africa. Despite the hurt and the political system, we can't hold a grudge. We must move on." Impulse—and God—made the six o'clock news that night.

We drove the group to Dallas, Texas, where they proudly cast their votes at the South African consulate. Reporters showed up to mark that event too, and Impulse responded with the patriotic song *"Nkosi Sikelei' iAfrika"* (Zulu for "God Bless Africa"). It became the South African national anthem in 1997.

Traveling together provided a priceless opportunity to enjoy fellowship with our South African friends. I opened for Impulse throughout the tour and sang a song written by Danny Daniels called "El Salvador." It has a country feel. Half the lyrics are translated into Spanish, making for quite a cultural contrast with Impulse's music. Soon our friends had learned it. During the long hours on the road, they sang "El Salvador"—and ate a lot of Kentucky Fried Chicken. It was a blending of cultures that no doubt was a delight to God!

CHAPTER 21

A Painful Path
to Multiplication

"All endings are also beginnings.
We just don't know it at the time."

—Mitch Albom, *The Five People You Meet in Heaven*

Youth With A Mission was hitting its stride by the early '90s.
Founder Loren Cunningham understood the necessity
of multiplication. Soon, scores of ministries rooted
in YWAM's three-pronged approach of training, evangelism,
and mercy ministry were reproducing worldwide. The training
was essential. So YWAM leaders launched the University of
the Nations (UofN), a biblically based university dedicated to
fulfilling the Great Commission.

Based on Holy Spirit guidance and the academic wisdom
of Dr. Howard Malmstadt, the UofN developed a modular
education system and live-learn environment that set it apart from
other universities. The international campus network brought
together multicultural and multigenerational staff and students—

worshiping, studying, praying, dining, and playing together in Christ-centered communities.

Because of my music education background and professional career, I recognized the need for Musicians for Missions to do more training. MFM provided a platform for music evangelism. But while our recruits had great zeal for God and music, some lacked the knowledge and experience they needed to fulfill their visions. We remedied this through in-house staff training in sound systems, recording, and touring, but we needed to do more.

Through Loren's vision for growth, I could see how UofN schools could enhance MFM's ability to prepare musicians for ministry. I received an invite to be on the ad hoc committee for developing the university's College of the Arts. The college opened a doorway through which Christian musicians and artists could get the schooling they needed for ministry and linked them to exciting international ministry opportunities.

I had worked with Jimmy and Carol Owens years before as they developed their School of Music Ministry. Their curriculum focused on engaging the church in worship. Whenever I taught in their school, I brought with me an added focus on missions. I learned so much from the Owenses and their administrator, Diane Wigstone, as I helped with their schools in Texas, Singapore, Hungary, and South Africa. My early Maranatha! training had fit hand in glove with YWAM's training structure for the launch of Musicians for Missions. Now, the design of Jimmy and Carol's school provided a template for developing a training school within YWAM that could take the MFM vision to a broader international level through the UofN.

We named our new course the School of Music in Missions (SOMM). We combined teaching from the Owenses' model with the elements of intercession and small group discipleship common to all YWAM schools. The SOMM emphasized music training, evangelism, and music production. My music education degree (which I had earlier thought I'd earned for no reason) now gave me insights that helped shape the SOMM curriculum. It was gratifying to finally offer a full-length training course instead of just seminars and individual events.

The curriculum would prepare students to handle their ministry professionally and uprightly before the Lord. We would teach musicians to seek God and understand their calling. Then we would equip them with the tools they needed to live it out. We launched the first SOMM in Amsterdam in 1995. YWAM musicians from several nations participated in that first school. Some students went on outreach to India and Eastern Europe, and others joined in ministry with the mercy ship *Caribbean Mercy.* Our goal was to multiply the school to other nations. The SOMM would expand to the United States, Australia, Latvia, and India in the next few years.

The School of Music in Missions became a valuable ministry gateway for musicians. It contributed to Musicians for Missions' growth in a way that hadn't happened during the Amsterdam years. As our relationship with international SOMM students grew, a worldwide network of musicians began to emerge. It later required a paradigm shift in my music ministry and leadership approach.

The School of Music in Missions fulfilled my dream to see musicians serving effectively in missions worldwide. But I had to start it outside of the very YWAM Amsterdam family that had once championed my vision for it. As with YWAM International, our base was also undergoing a painful transformation in the '90s. It began with Floyd and Sally McClung's transition from their leadership role and the emergence of a new leadership team. I had complete confidence in the members of the new team. They had long supported the development of MFM. So it was a shock to me to return to Holland from a ministry trip to find YWAM Amsterdam headed in a radically altered direction.

At that time, many diverse ministries were operating under the YWAM Amsterdam covering. I served on the base leadership council, but I was away and missed the critical meeting when they decided to restructure totally. Council members had concluded that some mobile ministries were growing independent and not providing their converts with adequate follow-up. YWAM, like other international ministries, had begun targeting specific cities and nations to achieve more focused ministry and enduring fruit. After prayer and discussion, YWAM Amsterdam's leadership team decided to follow suit. They chose to confine the base's ministry thrust to two areas: Urban Frontiers ministry (directed at specific cities and nations) and YWAM Amsterdam's local outreaches and ministries. This decision effectively cut off MFM and other existing ministries because their structures and emphases didn't meet the new criteria. MFM ceased to exist as a ministry under the YWAM Amsterdam umbrella.

MFM staff musicians now had to fit into either Urban Frontiers ministry or local Amsterdam ministry even though we wanted to continue doing both. We were already ministering in the base's target cities, but we were also getting invitations from other countries and cities. The decision to change direction forced us to decline those invitations.

The YWAM Amsterdam community launched into months of prayer and discussion. We rewrote our objectives to fit the new directive. MFM staff members also sought God about how we could fit in without losing our vision. Our family of musicians had always made a conscious effort to serve the base's larger vision. We pleaded with our leaders. *Hadn't we actively participated in everything that went on at YWAM Amsterdam? Hadn't we served its various ministries? Couldn't they see that our concerts outside Amsterdam helped keep a YWAM presence in front of the Dutch public?*

Our leaders listened but insisted we conform to the new structure. It was a painful, disappointing time. I felt misunderstood and underappreciated. With MFM dissolved, there was no longer a place or context for the spiritual and practical discussion that needed to happen amongst the musicians. I was no longer their leader, so there was no one to oversee their development and direction. Occasionally someone from the leadership team would ask me what kind of care the musicians required. They were discovering for themselves that musicians have particular spiritual and physical needs. Our people tried hard to fit into the new paradigm. Some adjusted well; others left altogether.

For me, it was as if they were taking my children away from me. For a season, I carried hurt and bitterness about how I believed they had treated me. I accepted the base's new direction but felt slighted that MFM didn't have a place in it. After much prayer, it became clear that I couldn't abandon the calling God had put on my heart for MFM. I approached the leadership team with my conclusion and a proposition, knowing this would be a make-or-break meeting.

"I'm called to serve all of YWAM as well as local churches," I began, "and to network with other organizations and facilitate other musicians as they discover where they're to serve. Those who are musicians don't just make music on the side—it's our full-time calling. That is why I joined YWAM and came to Holland in the first place."

"My call," I went on, "is stronger than the vision I'm trying to fit into right now at YWAM Amsterdam. If my calling no longer fits here, I regretfully will have to leave; but I would love to continue as part of YWAM and work out of Amsterdam. So, would you consider letting me run the MFM office and programs here—like a ministry within a ministry or a base within a base? To continue pursuing what I've been doing for the last twelve years?"

The leaders prayerfully considered my request. They released me to relaunch MFM as a separate YWAM ministry and generously allowed me and a handful of MFM musicians to continue at De Poort, which already housed our office and practice rooms. But those of us who made the shift would no longer have the supervision and covering of YWAM Amsterdam's leaders. It was not an easy transition. I had to form a leadership team and board and recruit staff. It was a lonely time for me, as I preferred the oversight and support of strong leadership.

God did not abandon me during the months that followed. He carried me like the Good Shepherd that he is, preparing me even in times of discouragement for the multiplication that was to come. We gave ourselves a new name—Musicians for Missions International (MFMI)—and prepared to launch the School of Music in Missions.

Some years later, I would go through counseling that helped me come to genuine peace about what happened in Amsterdam, forgiving those involved and reconciling with base leaders. In the end, it was another lesson in understanding that God's ways are not our ways—his ways are always about redemption in the face of difficult situations.

CHAPTER 22

Burnout and Beyond

"Success is not final, and failure is not fatal:
it is the courage to continue that counts."

—Winston S. Churchill

M usicians for Missions International experienced four years of fruitful ministry following the transition away from YWAM Amsterdam. We launched the School of Music in Missions in 1995. We served in the newly freed nations of Eastern Europe, conducted tours and music seminars, and participated in the Barcelona Olympics outreach in Spain. Despite these successes, I believe I stayed four years too long in Amsterdam, trying to make MFMI work in an isolated context. Our staff still served the Amsterdam base in many ways, but without their oversight or fellowship.

I was already a candidate for burnout by the time we launched the SOMM. What was supposed to have been the triumphal launch of an exciting new UofN course instead turned out to be one of my most dismal failures in leadership. I had never led a school before, and with no template, outside counsel, or supervision, that first school was nearly the death of me.

The staff consisted of eight talented professionals, most of whom I'd known for years. The friend I recruited to help run the school was an excellent leader in her own right, but we had different leadership styles that often clashed. Some school staff followed my lead wonderfully. Others came with their ideas of how to run the SOMM. The students benefitted from our staff's different giftings, but I received criticism over disputes within the staff team. And as hard as I tried, I couldn't handle some of the problems that arose.

At the end of that first school, Stan Pettengill and I were supposed to clean up and get reorganized. I knew Stan was planning to transition into another ministry. Still, I expected him to help close out this project first. When he informed me he would not help because he was already moving on, I blew up.

Looking back, I can't blame Stan for wanting to get out of working with me in light of all the conflict during the school. But I was hurting then, and I did what hurting people do—I lost it, reacting like a little girl. To me, this was one more instance in which a man left me to do the heavy work. As a woman, I was tired by then of carrying the load by myself. Through the filter of my insecurities, I had seen numerous times when men could have helped me but didn't. My falling-out with Stan was so severe it took me a year and some counseling to try to reconcile.

When Stan and I finally sat down over coffee to talk, I didn't know how to begin to ask his forgiveness. I was prepared to say, *I'm so sorry I didn't have the wisdom to lead all of you and that I hurt you because of it.* But before I could say anything, Stan said,

"I was such a jerk during the SOMM! How did you work with me? Please forgive me." Instead of finger-pointing, we humbled ourselves before each other right then and there, beginning a conversation that brought healing to our relationship.

My life had reached a critical point. I couldn't go on as I had, and I didn't know what to do next. Should I leave YWAM? Go home? Or somehow disappear? Worse, my mother's health was failing, and some of my former sexual issues were trying to raise their ugly heads. I was so broken and desperate that I would have done *anything* to find healing. Mercifully, by God's grace, pain and brokenness can drive us to a place where he can accomplish deep, lasting work in our lives.

I once heard a YWAM teacher say that if you focus on yourself, you'll get discouraged. If you focus on others, you'll get frustrated, and you'll get overwhelmed if you focus on the task. But if you focus on Jesus, you'll get empowered.

All I had to do was concentrate on Jesus. As I stepped aside from public ministry to do this, the Lord engineered one of the most significant healing times I ever experienced.

Shortly after the conclusion of that first SOMM, I attended a UofN workshop in Restenas, Sweden. While there, someone told me about Healing for the Nations, a retreat for Christian leaders going through spiritual, moral, or emotional crises. I leaped at the opportunity and made plans to go. I was so desperate that, for once, I didn't even worry about the credit card bill that I ran up as I flew from Amsterdam to Colorado to attend the retreat for a week. I could pay off credit cards, but my life couldn't wait.

The Navigators' scenic Glen Eyrie Conference Center in Colorado Springs, Colorado, hosted the retreat. Just being surrounded by God's beauty helped me feel his healing love right away. At the retreat, I came face-to-face with strongholds and lies born out of old hurts, fears, and a sense of abandonment. I learned that God is not the cause of pain and trouble in our lives. These result from sin in our fallen world, and God is there grieving *with* us during those painful, destructive events.

Whether we are victims of other peoples' actions or our own bad decisions, our hurt and fear perpetuate bitterness, deceptive self-images, and destructive choices. My counselors gently led me back to my fears' birthplaces, helping me identify them and cut off the root of bitterness. First, I had to identify the lies I had taken to heart and then exchange truth for those lies. The Word says, "You will know the truth, and the truth will set you free" (John 8:32 NIV).

One of the biggest lies I had accepted was that I didn't matter to men. As the retreat progressed, my counselors led me back to the origins of that falsehood, beginning with the earliest event: feeling abandoned by my father when he died unexpectedly. Although he had been a loving father, deep down, I'd always harbored the question: *Why did Daddy love alcohol more than me, his little girl?*

Because I had been the victim of inappropriate advances and sexual abuse at the hands of *some* men, I'd taken to heart a second lie. I believed that *most* of the men who pursued me only wanted to use and discard me. It also seemed that men disappeared when there was work to be done throughout my ministry years. I came to believe *I was nobody's priority*. Those memories had made me afraid to pursue long-term relationships with men.

The people in my life who seemed to care about me were women, and in those early cases, what started as good friendships turned into unnatural attachments. I have had many healthy, long-term friendships with women that didn't involve sexual attraction. But those early relationships went awry because, like me, my friends had needs and longings that went unfulfilled in their relationship with God or companionship with men. (See "My Healing Journey" in the back of this book for more about my healing process and freedom.)

I had let fear and lies rob me of the potential for genuine love in a male/female relationship. As I revisited memories and past experiences, the Holy Spirit helped me see how God grieved over each painful thing that had happened to me as a girl and as a woman. I had to choose forgiveness and decide to cut off the root of bitterness resulting from each incident. This process enabled me to restore my relationship with some men against whom I had held resentment. One was my brother, Walter, whom I had avoided for years. Unexpectedly, he acknowledged his abuse of me and asked my forgiveness. I was so thankful he took the initiative to make things right between us. That healing in our relationship paved the way for him to become a fatherly figure to me in his later years.

The Colorado retreat brought me much healing and freedom, but God wasn't done with me yet. He wanted to give me a whole new point of view. I went to Healing for the Nations feeling like a failure at life, but God showed me that this was no longer my identity. In my devotions one morning, I read the parable of the prodigal son. Suddenly, God spoke straight to my heart, saying, *Karen, I want you to get a ring. I want to give you a diamond ring as a token of my love. It has no other use than to represent how much I love you.*

I was stunned. I knew God loved me, but I had never received anything like this from him before. If he had given me a new guitar, I could have "given back" by using it for him. A ring has no other purpose than to be an extravagant expression of love. This gift was his act of pure love, no strings attached.

Amsterdam is known as the City of Diamonds, and I knew I could get a lovely diamond there. But I wondered how I would pay for it. While I was still at the retreat, I called Paul, who was taking care of my finances at the time. He informed me I had just received a big royalty check, much larger than usual. God had already provided for the ring he wanted to give me!

God still wasn't finished. During another morning devotional at the retreat, part of Isaiah 54:11 caught my eye: "O afflicted one, storm-tossed, and not comforted . . ." That's what I had felt like for years! I read on: "I will . . . lay your foundations with sapphires" (RSV). I knew the Lord was resetting my foundation at the retreat. He wanted me to have a diamond *and* sapphires to represent the new foundation he was laying for me.

When I returned to Amsterdam after the retreat, my friend Kelly Willard was visiting. She joined me in my search for a diamond. I learned that some diamonds appear perfect but have hidden flaws. I could identify with that! When they showed me a small but flawless diamond, I knew it was the right one.

I traveled to New Mexico and shared what God had asked me

to do with my sisters that Christmas. They conspired to be part of God's gift by giving me two beautiful rubies. I believe they heard rubies instead of sapphires because, just as the blood of Christ perfected me, those rubies made the diamond perfect.

The rubies and sapphires provided the foundation for my flawless diamond. God asked me always to wear the ring to symbolize his commitment to me. If I ever got married, I would give it to some single Christian woman to keep until she married. Then she would pass it on to some other unmarried woman as a token of God's perfect love.

We sometimes fail in life, but God never sees us as failures. Like the father of the prodigal son, God waited patiently, longing for me to learn from my failures and return to receive restored identity and relationship. This new, healthy perspective helped get me back on track as I sought the Lord regarding my next step.

CHAPTER 23

My Calling, My Tribe

Press on my friends to know him,
For to live is Christ, and we die to win.
Hold on to his words of promise;
Be his servant till the end.

—"I Have You in My Heart" by Karen Lafferty, from *Land of No Goodbyes*
© Heart Cry Music

Back in Amsterdam, YWAM friends embraced me with compassion and hope. As they prayed for me, my prophetic friend Christine delivered an intriguing word from the Lord to me:

"I've had many arrows for you before," she prophesied, "but now, your quiver is empty. I will fill it with new arrows." *New arrows?* I didn't understand what this meant yet, but it gave me confidence that God was moving me onward.

My calling to music and evangelism was still the same, but I knew some things had to change before I could continue. I laid my future and ministry on the altar as I waited for God to speak. Through additional counseling, I had come to see how self-driven and independent I had become while leading MFMI. I couldn't let that happen again.

The Lord directed me to establish criteria for future ministry, which would help me avoid my past negative behavior patterns. Four priorities emerged:

1. First, I needed to plug into a committed group of believers—a church, YWAM, or another ministry—for accountability and supportive relationships.
2. Second, I needed to be free to obey God's call to music and missions, traveling and ministering as he directed and helping to train music missionaries.
3. Third, I needed to spend several months a year helping my family take care of Mom as her health declined.
4. Finally, I needed to find and maintain a balance between traveling enough to accomplish my mission goals while being rooted in one place enough to develop healthy friendships.

I considered ministering out of the local church, but in my heart, I couldn't let go of YWAM. They were my tribe, and they had facilitated me and my ministry for years. And through the University of the Nations, there was significant potential to expand the MFMI vision internationally.

In February 1996, after reaffirming my connection with YWAM and establishing personal ministry criteria, I considered restarting MFMI. The YWAM Amsterdam leadership now recognized the need for a nurturing community for their musicians and invited me to work with them again. I contacted them to inquire about the future of MFMI and received this warm, generous response from Jim Mellis, one of the leaders:

> I want to affirm you in the way you are thinking about your next step (regarding a base location that both fits your ministry and your need for a home) and the initial direction you are feeling led. I could see you finding such a home in Amsterdam, but I agree with your assessment of your need to be able to give considerable care to your mother in the next couple of years. I feel positive about that and don't have much wisdom to add to what the Lord is already giving you. I would be open to any suggestions you have concerning a possible continuation of the ministry. My only question would be if there is not anyone to continue it, how do you feel if MFMI in Amsterdam "died" for a while as a seed in the ground? I'm not yet sure that will happen, but it is possible. Such seeds do come to life again. I've had it happen several times.

Jim's insightful response hit a nerve. Would I be willing to let MFMI die for a while or perhaps for good? I knew God could resurrect it anytime, anywhere, but there was no one in Amsterdam to help lead or staff it for the time being. My personal goal was to turn the leadership and organization over to others. I would travel and work with the growing international musician network. I didn't feel led to step back into my former role.

I attended a music and missions retreat with fellow Christian musicians Scott Wesley Brown, Byron Spradlin, Jimmy and Carol

Owens, Bobby Michaels, and others. I shared with them about my crossroads, and the prayer and counsel they offered me were both healing and helpful. Shortly after, I received attractive offers to work in Nashville and Virginia Beach in music and missions.

I considered these new scenarios. It dawned on me that the root of my unsettledness was the difficulty of serving elsewhere while also trying to help my mom in New Mexico. If I accepted any of the ministry options on the table, it meant coming home and living in my stepfather Paul's house as a "guest" while caring for Mom. To do that while trying to conduct the business of ministry would be both disruptive and draining.

Then one day, while I was studying Psalm 127, God began to speak to me, starting with the first verse: "Unless the Lord builds a house, they who build it labor in vain." The Scripture reminded me that God, not I, was the one who had to build the ministry. When I read in verses three and four that "children are a gift of the Lord . . . a reward . . . like arrows . . . so are the children of one's youth," I thought about my mom. The arrows caught my attention because so many prophetic words spoken over me called me an arrow. Verse 5 read: "Blessed is the man whose quiver is full of [arrows]; they will not be ashamed" (NASB). As Mom's children, God intended us to be a blessing to her and not cause her shame. As I thought back on the years she had given to us, the Lord spoke to me that it would not be right for us to shame her by not taking care of her at this time.

That was my answer. A move to Santa Fe fit all four criteria God had given me. My discouragement and lack of motivation washed away as God gave me visionary ideas for glorifying him in that beautiful, culturally diverse city. I started planning my move to Santa Fe with new enthusiasm, researching what it would take to incorporate YWAM and MFMI in that city.

Leaving Amsterdam was bittersweet. I had grown to love the city, the Dutch people, and the YWAM community. I had even obtained Dutch citizenship. I would miss the Dutch coffee, fresh *stroopwafels* (a thin waffle with sweet caramel sauce inside), Dutch cheeses, *patat frit* (French fries), and those cozy moments of *gezelligheid*.

It was important to me to say goodbye to people in Amsterdam and close that chapter well, so I threw myself a going-away party. I invited people I knew from around Holland and former coworkers from YWAM Holland. We celebrated the history of MFMI and all that God had done. The YWAM community blessed me, prayed for me, and honored me with a beautiful painting of Amsterdam.

I left with no bitter feelings or unresolved issues. Today I can share the hurts and difficult times I experienced because I have experienced healing and restoration. I have great respect for all the leaders I worked with, and I will always thank God for that rich season in my life.

CHAPTER 24

A Farewell to
My Biggest Fan

And we're singing the songs of the family;
And we've entered the dream of eternity
In the Land of No Goodbyes.

—"Land of No Goodbyes" by Karen Lafferty, from *Land of No Goodbyes*
© Heart Cry Music

Mom had been a steady light in my life. Now that light was flickering and growing dim. While I was in Amsterdam, my siblings regularly reported differences in her physical and emotional well-being. Whenever I came home, I saw these changes firsthand. Mom was getting shaky. It was hard for her to write, so she started typing everything. She began forgetting important things and having sharp mood swings.

One evening, at Mom and Paul's house in Ruidoso, I heard a plate shatter in the kitchen. Paul began yelling, so I rushed in to find out what was going on. Paul had said something uncomplimentary about the beans Mom had served him. In response, she had picked up the plate and thrown it across the room. We'd all been joking about her temper, but we couldn't explain this incident away as mere temper. Something was wrong.

We decided it was time to take Mom to Mayo Clinic for an evaluation. Two days of testing and X-rays revealed atrophy in the frontal lobes of her brain. Mom was diagnosed with Pick's Disease, a form of dementia in which the brain can't make associations or send signals. Doctors explained that victims might form ideas, but they can't express them. They eventually lose motor skills and find it difficult to speak.

All of these symptoms, plus more, manifested as the disease progressed. Mom would laugh at herself when she grabbed hold of things and couldn't let go. When she couldn't finish a sentence, we would jump in and help her. She often cried about being sick and unable to serve. Her lack of coordination kept her from doing the crafts and decorative projects she loved.

Paul was an impatient caregiver and too old to lift her or help her to the bathroom at night. So my sisters began a rotation of having Mom in their homes to ensure she had the care she needed. Eventually, we knew we had to put her in a nursing care facility. We chose a good one and reserved a room. But before the move, we sisters went out to lunch. We discussed it some more, and we couldn't bring ourselves to do it yet. We canceled the room and continued to move her between their homes for care.

I determined to move back from Amsterdam as quickly as possible. How could I not be there for my mom—the woman God had used to shape my life? Mom was the primary person responsible for me knowing the Lord. She had encouraged my pursuit of music, purchased my instruments, helped me when money was tight, and was always my biggest fan. Although I believe she had hoped for some measure of stardom for me, she was supportive of my call to music ministry. Even now, in her illness, God was using her to direct my life.

I'm so glad I moved back in that last year of her life. We finally put her in the nursing home in Los Alamos. One of us was always there to put her to bed rather than leaving that to the busy staff. We knew Mom's favorite lotions and all the things she liked that the caregivers couldn't know. We hoped that our personal touch would make her time there less impersonal and clinical. I had the sense that God was using us to ease Mom's way to her heavenly home.

Still, it was hard to leave Mom each night. She would hang onto us, and she wouldn't have let us go even if she could have gotten her muscles to cooperate. We made sure she had a visitor every day. For several months, most of my music ministry consisted of singing to her and the other nursing home residents. It's a good and needful ministry for these beautiful people; their bodies are wearing out, but their spirits are alive. Even in dementia, music could touch the deep places of their hearts when other things couldn't.

During Mom's last year, I took a few concert bookings. One day, while in Maine for concerts, I received a call from Fran informing me Mom had pneumonia and had lost her ability to swallow. "It doesn't look like she has long to live," she said. I returned home right away. My nephew Ken joined Fran, Satie, Paul, and me as we watched over Mom. Knowing the disease's progression, we had already talked with her about what she would want us to do when this inevitable time came. She told us just to let her go to be with Jesus.

Mom wasn't in pain thanks to medications, but we could probably say that she starved to death. She couldn't eat or even swallow water without choking and coughing. How hard it must have been for her!

Mom's earthly life came to a close on May 7, 1997, at La Residencia in Old Santa Fe. It was a beautiful spring day, and the aides had moved her to the third floor, where the family could be alone with her. That morning, sensing it would be her last day, we stepped out of the room so Paul, her husband of thirty-five years, could say his goodbyes. Then we returned and held her hands and worshiped, singing softly in her ear. Later that afternoon, her legs began turning dark, a sign that death was near.

Her breathing grew slower and slower. "Mom," I whispered to her, "It's okay. You can let go. Jesus is waiting for you." It seemed fitting that Mom was slipping away as we watched a beautiful New Mexico sunset. Then a gust of warm, high desert air blew in through the open window, ruffling her hair and filling her lungs for the last time. Her breathing stopped, and a peaceful stillness filled the room. The quiet broke as the bells of the Saint Francis Cathedral rang out, seeming to proclaim that the angels had just ushered the spirit of another saint into the presence of the Lord.

Paul turned to Satie, Fran, and me.

"I just want to thank you girls for how you always took care of your mom," he said. Then he broke down and cried. Fran—who had never accepted Paul as a father and had been angry about his impatience with Mom's frailty and disease—put her arms around him as he wept. It began a time of healing between them.

Now it was time for my final goodbye. Looking at Mom's still form, I thought to myself, *Mom used to live here, and now she is with the Lord.* When the hospice workers came to prepare the body, I had such peace that I could even help them roll her over.

We took her home to Alamogordo and buried her in a plot Paul had purchased for them both. A few years later, we buried Fran near the two of them.

I sang "Great Is Thy Faithfulness" as part of Mom's funeral service. Many friends and her children, including her stepson Jerry, gathered to honor her rich eighty-year life. Mom had been the family glue, and now that she was gone, we realized we would have to work at staying connected. We committed to honoring Mom by keeping in touch. Our family lives scattered throughout several states, but we've observed that commitment, sharing many happy memories since that time.

Thank you, God, for giving me this wonderful woman as my mother!

CHAPTER 25

Full Circle

"There is a kind of magicness about going away
and then coming back all changed."

—Kate Douglas Wiggin, *New Chronicles of Rebecca*

On my final flight back to New Mexico a year before my mom's passing, my mind flashed on the favorite sights and smells of my homeland. The high desert, the towering Sangre de Cristo Mountains, the clear blue skies, the star-studded nights—and the bright red, aromatic chiles hung to dry in the sun. I thought of the scent of sage hanging in the air before a summer rain and the spicy fragrances wafting from Mexican kitchens. Most of all, I thought about the people I would be with and ministering to in Santa Fe.

The words *santa fe* mean "holy faith" in Spanish. So it seemed natural that the four-hundred-year-old city that was now to be my home was a place that attracted seekers of spiritual truth. It was also a crossroads of culture, rich and warm with Spanish and Native American influences.

As I mused about my new life in Santa Fe during my flight, I realized that I had many Anglo and Hispanic friends there. But I didn't even have one Native American friend. Why? I concluded it was because we lived in different worlds. Opportunities for togetherness and friendship didn't come naturally. I was uncomfortable with that. My mission work took me to many nations. I loved the uniqueness and creativity of other cultures, and I learned so much from them. Before my plane landed in Albuquerque, I had determined that ministering to and with the Pueblo, Apache, Navajo, and other tribes in our area would be one of my focuses as I established a new life in New Mexico. The possibilities excited me!

One of our Foundational Values in YWAM is that we work in teams. I sought the Lord concerning who would partner with me. He brought Sandy and Julia Hoffman to mind. We had worked together during Jimmy and Carol Owens' Music Ministry School in Budapest in 1992. They had also helped me staff the SOMM in Amsterdam. We were comfortable as friends and in ministry.

Sandy and Julia worked for several years at Last Days Ministries in Texas, founded by contemporary Christian musician Keith Green and his wife, Melody. Keith died in a tragic plane crash in 1982. Although Melody continued with the ministry after his death, she now felt it was time to move from Texas. With Last Days' imminent closure, the Hoffmans were praying about their next step when I contacted them. To my joy, they readily accepted my invitation to help pioneer YWAM Santa Fe. I knew they would add tremendous strength to the new work. We launched from an office set up in my garage, working alongside local churches on outreach activities.

When Sandy, Julia, and I started YWAM Santa Fe, our goals were to nurture the existing MFMI network, raise up contemporary musicians, and create special local music and arts events. Those would include concerts, schools, seminars, and hopefully, future art exhibits. As a mission organization, we would take both students and locals on mission trips as well. However, we knew we would have to do some new and different things to reach the Santa Fe community. The city was a prominent hub of the fine arts market in America. Sandy and I were musicians, and our first recruits were musicians. Still, we knew we also needed to pray for staff with other artistic skills.

Santa Fe was full of beautiful art, but I hadn't seen anything focused on the One who gives the beauty and truth we all desire. There was some religious art but nothing that brought out the character and nature of the Great Artist. I had a strong sense that God desired a center for the arts that expressed his truth about creativity, life, and relationships.

My heart began to beat for the redemption of arts and culture in Santa Fe, for redirecting those expressions to the Source of creativity. The center I had in mind would be an extension of the local church. It would be a place welcoming to all, where art and beauty would reflect our great God as well as a biblical worldview. From that platform, artists of every discipline could build relationships with each other and community art lovers. The center would also expose local churches to arts in ministry. It would eventually house an art gallery, performance space, coffee shop, and art school.

Before we could achieve our goals and ideas, YWAM Santa Fe needed to become a creative presence in the city. We initiated an events branch called Sangre de Cristo Arts (SCA) to demonstrate our art vision. The name fit in Santa Fe because it was the name of the mountains just east of the city and because it's Spanish for "blood of Christ." It was a standard, nonthreatening name yet significant. Years later, it was on my heart to include Christ-followers of various ethnic groups, so we added "culture" to the title. Through our creative offerings, Sangre de Cristo Arts and Culture would have an even broader assignment to help people discover the joy of Christ's love, truth, and beauty.

In December 1998, we produced a Santa Fe program to exemplify how we wanted to fulfill our vision. *Feliz Navidad New Mexico* (Merry Christmas New Mexico) featured Fernando Ortega, an award-winning contemporary singer, songwriter, and native New Mexico son. We also incorporated local talent to tell the story of Christmas through narration, Santa Fe traditions, song, and dance. *Feliz Navidad New Mexico* ran for two nights before packed houses at Santa Fe's James A. Little Theater.

We also strove to hold events designed to help people think about their relationship with God. We created a meditative worship concert billed as *Come to the Peace: A Personal Time with God.* The beautiful Loretto Chapel in downtown Santa Fe—with its "miracle" spiral staircase, stained-glass windows, and sculptured Stations of the Cross—was the perfect place for it. As people entered the sanctuary, we instructed them not to speak to one another but to focus on listening to God. We played soft, meditative music as readers shared encouraging Scriptures. Many visitors commented that it provided a place of refuge in their busy lives.

While I enjoyed our local outreach activities, I began thinking once again of ways to connect globally. I knew then that it was time to revisit the School of Music in Missions.

CHAPTER 26

Back in the Saddle

It's a place I can come home to,
A place I'd rather not leave,
A place I feel I belong to,
And a place that belongs to me.

—"New Mexico Song" by Karen Lafferty, from *Life Pages—Love of the Ages*
© Capitol Christian Music Group

YWAM Santa Fe was the logical place to reintroduce the School of Music in Missions. I was ready to "get back on my horse," having worked through the mistakes I'd made pioneering the school in Amsterdam. In September 1997, I gathered a staff team, arranging to host the school at the lovely Glorieta Conference Center, east of Santa Fe. Twenty students from eight nations arrived at the school.

We ran music training courses annually after that. Sometimes we conducted the five-month School of Music in Missions and sometimes the six-week Music Ministry Development Seminar. The University of the Nations network helped launch both schools at locations in the United States and abroad to accommodate international students better. Many of the staff and students became ministry partners. They carried the vision for music in missions to their nations and cultures.

We created a colorful, multicultural "Christmas Around the World Tour" outreach opportunity for our Santa Fe schools. Our students learned to develop their musical and communication skills. Audiences learned how other cultures received and expressed their faith in Christ. The tour became one of our most popular outreach events.

For one student named Allie, the tour rekindled love and hope for her native Ireland. She once told me she hated being from Northern Ireland. Allie had been living in England to disassociate herself from the religious troubles and violence back in Belfast. But the audiences' positive responses and affirmations touched her as she repeatedly shared how the gospel came to the Irish people.

When the tour was over, Allie approached me and said, "Karen, I'm sorry, but I don't think I'm supposed to go with the band on the outreach. I feel I'm supposed to go home and let God use me to help bring reconciliation between Catholics and Protestants." Her change of heart reflected the kind of results we prayed our schools would bring! We blessed Allie and sent her on her way.

Kima Fanai, our first student from India, attended our initial SOMM in Amsterdam. We formed a band around him to do campus evangelism in Pune, India. When I paid the band a pastoral visit, they booked a concert for me. I had never felt called to India. But once I got involved and saw the incredible potential, I was hooked.

I did a tour of my own in India, ending up at YWAM Bangalore, where I played a short concert at the campus. There was no mic stand, so Benny Prasad, one of the DTS students, held the mic for me. Afterward, he asked, "Can you teach me that song, 'Jesus in Your Heart'?"

"Well, I'm leaving early tomorrow morning, right after breakfast," I told him.

"Okay then, right before breakfast?" He was determined to learn!

Once I saw Benny's talent and motivation, I invited him to attend our School of Music in Missions in Santa Fe. Part of the school's teaching centers on translating our dreams into a plan and timeline and setting concrete goals to reach our objectives. By the end of his schooling, Benny's goal was to hold the SOMM in India. I committed to lead that first school in Bangalore in 2001 with Benny as my assistant.

Benny went on to become a highly proficient musician. His extraordinary determination and musicianship enabled him to set the world record for traveling to every nation in the world in the shortest amount of time. Wherever Benny goes, he shares the gospel, plays concerts, meets presidents and dignitaries, and befriends well-known musicians along the way. As his international renown grows, one thing remains the same: Benny does it all for the love of Jesus.

◈

My life has grown rich working with other cultures. It now has grown even richer serving among Native Americans in New Mexico. I began making trips to the Jemez Pueblo to attend meetings at HWY 4 Zion, a monthly gathering of believers filled with song, testimonies, teaching, and fellowship. I met six women, ranging in age from eleven to eighty, who sang in the native Towa language. Frank Shendo, the father of two sisters in the group, wrote the songs they sang. His name in Towa was *Waa-Haa-Mee-Nee* (wǎ hǎ mē nē), meaning "Cloud Racer."

Waa-Haa-Mee-Nee wrote many praise songs after he and his wife became Christians in the 1960s. Some were translations of the hymns he was learning. Some were original songs in Towa, written in the traditional Native American style. The Jemez Pueblo women sang these songs in simple unison, accompanied by one drum.

Carmelita, leader of the Waa-Haa-Mee-Nee Singers, often said, "One day, we're going to record these songs."

"Let's do it!" I said.

It was an honor to guide the Waa-Haa-Mee-Nee ladies through their project. Their CD, completed in 2015 with local friends' support, provided an excellent way for these women to share their faith with others at the Jemez Pueblo. Since Towa is not a written language, their songs and the spoken Word enable them to reach their people effectively.

Over the years, God sent vital people to help develop YWAM Santa Fe's multifaceted ministry: musicians, songwriters, photographers, office workers, school staff, and event managers.

Some came from as far away as Africa, Asia, and Europe, bringing their unique cultural flavor to our local outreaches and our international network. I was gratified to see multiple arts ministries blossom during the many years I served on the University of the Nations College of Arts & Sports committee. And my missionary spirit has been kept alive through taking church teams to Honduras and small groups to Australia, New Zealand, Africa, and across the US.

Yet, we were still missing a crucial element—we needed a visual artist to come who understood the fine arts heart in Santa Fe. I was overjoyed when I received an inquiry about a YWAM staff position from Marianne Millar, a fine arts professional. She first showed her paintings of Native Americans in Santa Fe galleries. When Marianne joined our staff, it rounded out our pool of artists. It opened new ministry possibilities, taking us a step closer to fulfilling our vision for Sangre de Cristo Arts and Culture.

I am forever grateful to each of these gifted people for their service in YWAM Santa Fe. As we continue to pursue arts-related ministry opportunities, I still actively pray and watch for open doors toward developing a Christian arts center in Santa Fe. Other people have begun to capture the vision as well. I don't know if the Lord will use me or others to reach the people of Santa Fe with his truth through beauty and art, but I do know this: The people of Santa Fe are searching for God's love, peace, and beauty. Artistic expressions created by people who have experienced the depth of God's love can reach deep into others' souls and heal their pain. Connecting those expressions with the peoples' needs drives my prayer for the city of Santa Fe.

Whenever people ask me what is next for me, I tell them that I'm home in New Mexico to stay as far as I know. I always knew I would come back and live here one day. New Mexico is still "the place I can come home to." I want to continue playing and singing the Lord's songs for as long as I am able. I remain committed to music and art evangelism and helping as many people as possible to catch the vision. I intend to fan the flame of the next generation of Christian musicians and artists, whether they are here in Santa Fe, around the United States, or across the ocean.

I sometimes wonder about what is coming or how long my health will hold up. But when worry tempts me, the Lord reminds me again of Matthew 6:33. Then I know one thing for sure: Whatever lies ahead, if I seek the Lord, he will be there for me.

Epilogue

I t's a joy to say that I am comfortable where I'm at in life now. I am older and wiser, and I am convinced that this is the place God wants to take us all. In Proverbs 2:9–11, Solomon records the promise made to those who trust in the Lord: "Then you will understand what is right, just, and fair, and you will find the right way to go. For wisdom will enter your heart, and knowledge will fill you with joy. Wise choices will watch over you. Understanding will keep you safe" (NLT). While I am far from perfect, God is perfecting me through Christ. I better understand God's grace, his ways, and who I am as I walk in them.

If I knew back when I was twenty-five what I know now, I would have received counseling sooner on some painful issues in my life. I would have practiced more and taken better care of my ears (we're foolish about those things when we're young). Some people thought it was a mistake to abandon a promising music career and pursue European missions. But that was no mistake. I saw a wide-open opportunity to reach youth worldwide with contemporary Christian music. God compelled me to go and bring as many willing musicians with me as possible. My work with MFM created many lasting friendships. I've had the privilege of watching young musicians I mentored grow into mature leaders.

In hindsight, I can see that I developed Musicians for Missions International too much around Karen Lafferty rather than the more encompassing ministry I'd envisioned. I wish I could say MFMI had fifty bases around the world. But I am grateful for the many people we have trained and launched into missions. I would love for MFMI to be active beyond my lifetime.

I once asked God what I was supposed to be—a musician first or a leader and facilitator of others. His answer was *both*. I'm glad I had the sense to follow what I felt God was telling me rather than the voice of a handful of people. Instead of regrets, I have the deep satisfaction of not only hearing from God but seeing people I invested in going out and ministering in music.

Even though I never had the joy of being married or physically birthing children, I am happy when my "spiritual children" succeed. I understand what the apostle Paul felt when he wrote in 1 Thessalonians 2:19–20: "For who is our hope or joy or crown of exultation? Is it not even you, in the presence of our Lord Jesus at His coming? For you are our glory and joy" (NASB1995). Or 1 Thessalonians 3:8: "For now we really live, if you stand firm in the Lord" (NASB1995).

When I moved back to the States, I thought I might reconnect with friends and colleagues from the Jesus movement days. It didn't happen. It may have been different had I moved back to California instead of New Mexico. I had a second-fiddle feeling when I didn't receive an invitation to some of the Jesus movement reunion concerts. But I don't think it was intentional.

No doubt, many were overlooked because of the sheer number of people involved in those days. Then the Lord reminded me that long ago, he moved me into a much larger international family. He brought to mind the many festivals and significant mission events I played at around the world. I would not have had the chance to do those if I had remained in California.

Despite some disappointments and what-ifs, I've seen God's loving hand of grace, discipline, guidance, healing, and adventure. My work with churches and YWAM has given me an abundance of close friends and coworkers from other countries and cultures. I've served with many incredible people whom I will forever hold in my heart. Some are my actual blood relatives, but many are as close as family because of our shared life experiences and long-term commitment to one another.

If anything could be said of me, I hope it would be that I've always tried to seek the kingdom of God first. More than ever, I believe the most important thing we can do is listen for the voice of God, wait for the prompting of the Holy Spirit, then do what he asks us to do. If we do these things, he will add all the things we need.

A Word to Musicians

I believe God wants all aspects of our human experience to reflect him. His gift of music is one way he touches the deepest places of the human soul. As Christian musicians, we have the privilege of bringing life-giving moments to people, but this gift can be a snare to us if not used with the right spirit. Allow me to share some of the profound truths and joys I've discovered while living as one of God's troubadours.

Perhaps the essential truth concerns our *identity*. We all tend to view who we are through the lens of our gender, nationality, race, economic status, physical appearance, talents, relationships, and so on. You may discover early in life that you have the talent to be a musician. That's a gift from God, but it doesn't define who you are or give you *value*.

God's love is what makes us valuable, not our abilities and accomplishments. He loves us so much that through Jesus Christ, he provided a way for us to dwell in his holy presence forever. Understanding this truth frees us to enjoy fully being musicians. Getting people to notice us, selling more recordings, or outperforming others no longer drives us. Being a musician is part of who we are, but it isn't our chief identity.

Those called to music recognize that God uses us as his instruments to bring joy, beauty, healing, and hope to a needy world.

Growing in my understanding of the purpose and effect of music has also been vital in my life. I love beautiful instrumental music; it's probably what motivated me to take up instruments early in life. The purity of an oboe, the worshipful call of a Native American flute, the velvety warmth of a cello, the lonely cry of a blues saxophone. A well-played acoustic guitar, rhythms that make us dance, the tapestry of a full orchestra. These all bring an array of colors to enhance our life journey.

A Christian man once told me, "Music is worthless without words." I challenged him with the story of how the evil spirits fled when David ministered to Saul by simply playing music on his lyre—wordless music. Music produces heartfelt emotions and often peace and comfort. David and Saul—as well as the evil spirits—understood this. As it has done to everything else in life, man's fall has distorted music (perhaps Lucifer had something to do with that since he was a musician). But God created music to be part of the abundant life he intends for us.

While flying home one time, I sat next to an American who told me he was a Buddhist. He was headed to Santa Fe to help conduct a conference on aesthetics. As we talked, he was pleased that I was also interested in aesthetics and asked why. I told him I was a musician seeking to create music that would reflect beauty and believed God was the creator of aesthetics. When God breathed the breath of life into us, he imparted his love of beauty with it.

"An interesting perspective!" the man said. "Would you be willing to come to our conference as an artist in residence and share your perspective?" Unfortunately, I had a scheduling conflict, but I hoped he would give further thought to the concept I had given him.

"Why do we hunger for beauty?" is the question Jim Croegaert asks in his song of the same title. Even when ugliness surrounds us, music can comfort the weary soul. Musicians are blessed to have the power to bring beauty and joy into not-so-beautiful places.

Years ago, several YWAM leaders accompanied a doctor making the rounds of a YWAM refugee camp along the Cambodian border. He was assessing the needs of the desperate refugees and developing strategies to help them. One of the men in the group slid the guitar he was carrying under a table as the doctor briefed them. The doctor noticed this and said, "Young man, these people need the healing you can bring with that guitar as much as they need my healing." The power of that statement stuck with me.

Music is a healing balm that prisoners, refugees, the hopeless, and the sick need in addition to having their practical needs met. I've watched prisoners abandon themselves to music, finding fullness and joy in the presence of the Lord (Psalm 16:11). We bring part of God's heart and beauty into peoples' colorless lives by presenting music that pleases and touches the senses.

In Matthew 25:31–46, Jesus teaches us the importance of comforting those who are suffering. We who are musicians must recognize that God's intent for music is to bless others. While *we* get joy and satisfaction from playing music, we should also do it to help others.

My approach is often to play something people can identify with that will touch their hearts. It may be a song about friendship, or a mother's love, or how the night sky gives them peace (since even nature declares the glory of God). But that's not the whole story. People need to hear the words of the gospel, about how God sent his Son to die for them, about sin and repentance, and God's justice and mercy. We must tell the whole account of Jesus' death and resurrection so others might discover that "old things are passed away; behold, all things are become new" (2 Corinthians 5:17 KJV).

As musicians, we need to seek creative ways to convey this. Our songs are often just a stepping stone, a moment of enlightenment for the listener. Seek to give them something that touches their soul, something they will think about in their quiet hours. As we sing the truth, God's Spirit will speak to their human spirit, and people will experience something they can't explain, yet they will know it is real.

At times, wordless music *sets the stage* for the presentation of the gospel through the spoken Word. But many people also come to faith through songs that express the good news through music and lyrics. We find songs of faith throughout the Scriptures, and I believe God would have us continue that musical tradition to honor him, proclaim his truths, and encourage one another.

Some years back, a friend in Amsterdam was dying from bone cancer. I took my guitar and went to visit him in the hospital. His family stood around his bed, and they asked if I would sing something that would speak to him. I sang "Love of the Ages" by John Wytock. It tells the story of the Lamb that was slain for our sins so we could have eternal life. The family joined me in the final chorus:

And we'll all live together in the house of the Lord;
And we'll all live forever,
Praise the Lord, praise the Lord!

After singing those triumphant words, we stood in peaceful silence, letting the incredible truth of it sink in. Several days later, my friend went home to be with the Lord. Whenever I sing that song now, I remember how bringing God's truth through music gave strength and hope to that family.

Some songs are like prayers. For me, Bob Bennett's song "You're Always Welcome Here" helps me be honest before God. Using the metaphor of our lives as a house, Bob writes:

'Cause when I cry, the roof leaks;
And when the wind blows, the walls are weak.
But a house is known by the company it keeps;
And I feel better now that you're near.
And I want to make it clear,
Jesus, from now on,
You're always welcome here.

Two powerful songs of faith that continually inspire me are "The Steadfast Love of the Lord" and "Great Is Thy Faithfulness" from Lamentations 3:22-23. The Scripture reads: "The steadfast love of the LORD never ceases; his mercies never come to an end; they are new every morning; great is your faithfulness" (ESV). These songs come from Jeremiah's account of a time when death and destruction were all around. I and countless others have sung these songs through tears and hard times. They encourage us to keep standing tall in our faith.

I've appreciated those who've written me about how one of my songs has spoken to them. Whether we're singing our song or someone else's, the music and the message should touch the listeners. If you have the ability and passion for songwriting, please don't neglect it. We need your songs!

My final word to musicians is to seek God diligently about where music fits into your life. For some, music may only be a part of what you do, not your primary focus. For others, God will call you to full-time music ministry. I can tell you from experience that a lifelong career in music ministry will be challenging. It will require you to grow in God's Word, learn how to minister through prayer and evangelism, raise support, be frugal, and live to serve others.

Whether you see music as your vocation or something else in your life, I pray you will never lose the joy that playing or listening to music was meant to bring. God may lead you to be one of his troubadours—bringing truth, joy, and beauty to this dark world that needs his grace so desperately. If so, I believe you will have no regrets and, in the end, will find it was a life well spent. May all your songs be birthed out of a relationship with our Father God.

My Healing Journey

It has taken a lot of courage to speak openly and honestly about my former struggles with same-sex attraction. Because it's such a big issue today, I felt I needed to share about how God lovingly led me into healing, understanding, and restoration. I am also aware that others with similar stories need a listening ear, compassion, and forgiveness.

I've learned a lot about same-sex attraction through the Word, books, counseling, and many conversations. Whenever I impart what I've learned to others, I always begin with the premise on which I believe my healing is based. That is the conviction of my sin through God's Word and submission to that Word.

I know many today adamantly maintain that being gay is not a choice. I would have agreed at one point in my life. I have since realized that almost anyone, given certain circumstances, could turn to the same sex for love. What changed my mind was considering the real possibility that what happened to me influenced my thinking, emotions, and choices.

My healing began as I grew deeper in my love for God and my desire to please him. Quite honestly, I also realized how much God had invested in me. If I didn't turn this area of my life over to him, I would risk losing the ministry he had given me. Even worse, I would bring shame to his name. I felt trapped at first. *God, why do I have these attractions for women if it's not what you want for me? It's unfair. Don't you want me to have love in my life?* After much wrestling with God over a long period, I concluded that even if giving up same-sex relationship meant I would not have physical love in my life, it was worth giving it up for God's love. For some, this cost seems too great.

Mine is a testimony of God's mercy and faithfulness. I didn't know at first if my emotions would ever change. But I knew I had to follow his path to have any peace in my life. So I began trusting in God rather than my emotions—this was key. God brought about my restoration through compassionate counseling, his deep love, and the acceptance and affirmation I received from others.

As I believed God and moved forward, two important things occurred. First, I realized I was no longer experiencing unhealthy attractions toward new women friends. More recently, I also found myself attracted to a male friend. That attraction was huge for me. It was a sign that following God's ways could bring my innermost being into line with his Word.

I am over seventy as I write this book and may never have the pleasure of being married. But just knowing that my emotions are in the right place gives me a lot of peace. I am grateful to God for his restoration. I pray my testimony will prevent some from falling into this trap or help others get out of it.

I have great compassion for those who feel this lifestyle is their lot in life and have resolved that they are gay. I won't reject or judge them because God is their judge, not I. I will genuinely love them.

I have learned that humankind's problem is not a particular sexual sin. *All* of us have the sin problem. It comes in various forms, and we all have to deal with it. It's never easy. Those of us who choose to deal with the sin issue will find Someone who will rescue us—Jesus. We will never regret surrendering to his love and receiving his mercy.

However, in today's society, the gay lifestyle is widely accepted. Those like me who choose to believe what God says about relationships instead of listening to their emotions are considered intolerant. But I know that God will walk this healing path with anyone choosing to pursue it. God *is* a God of understanding and comfort. "You will know the truth, and the truth will set you free" (John 8:32 NIV).

I encourage you to study this further. The following references may help you personally or help you love and minister to others who identify with LGBTQ. Links to teaching videos are available on my website, *https://karenlafferty.com/Seek-Ye-First-Book*, and I also recommend the following books:

- *Sing Over Me* by Dennis Jernigan
- *Washed and Waiting: Reflections on Christian Faith* by Wesley Hill
- *The Secret Thoughts of an Unlikely Convert* by Rosario Butterfield and Russell Moore

Glossary

CASA—Christian Artists South Africa, a training seminar modeled after Cam Floria's original US-based Christian Artists Seminar (see **CAS** for expanded definition)

CAS—Christian Artists Seminar, a training seminar offered by Christian Artists (an international association of over one hundred organizations). Christian Artists started in the 1960s with the Continental Singers, who traveled many nations and gave impetus to creative and spiritual renewal. Their success led to the formation of the annual Christian Artists Seminar (1974–1999 with Cam Floria in the Colorado Rockies, USA) and the annual Christian Artists Seminar in Europe (1980–1981 and continuing).

DTS—Discipleship Training School, YWAM's entry-level training program

MSOS—Musicians Summer of Service, a YWAM summer outreach program

SCAC—Sangre de Cristo Arts and Culture, the expanded events branch of YWAM Santa Fe, NM

SCA—Sangre de Cristo Arts, the original events branch of YWAM Santa Fe, NM

SOMM—School of Music in Missions, a music and missions training school offered by YWAM

SOS—Summer of Service, a YWAM summer outreach program

UofN CAS—University of the Nations College of Arts & Sports

UofN—University of the Nations (Kona, HI), part of YWAM

YWAM—"Youth With A Mission is *a global movement of Christians from many cultures, age groups, and Christian traditions dedicated to serving Jesus throughout the world.* Also known as YWAM (pronounced 'WHY-wham'), we unite in a common purpose to know God and to make Him known."

In Memory

I want to honor my family, friends, and other significant people who have gone on to be with the Lord. Whether I've mentioned them in my story or not, each one played a meaningful and transformative role in my life. I loved them all for who they were, and I will never forget them. To read more about them, please visit my website at *www.KarenLafferty.com/Seek-Ye-First-Book*.

Walter Lafferty Sr. • Ollie Lafferty Stout Brown • Fran Lafferty Bunker • Walter Lafferty Jr. and Margaret • Satie Lafferty Hamberg • Paul F. Brown • Betty Lafferty • Herb Brunell • Satie Stout (Grandma Stout) • Rock Lafferty • Rhonda Ray Wilkenson • Pastor Chuck (Papa Chuck) and Kay Smith • Pastor Romaine • Pastor John Wimber • Ted Bleymeyer • Tom Stipe • Bobby Michaels • Tiffany Walters • Stan Pettengill • Bill Sprouse • Roby Duke • Larry Hefty • Keith Green • Duduzile Thafeni • Bud Lang • Marilyn Gruska • Corrie ten Boom • Belarmino "Blackie" Gonzalez and daughter Annette Garcia • Diana Hamm • Marie Benson • Philippe Bogdon • Virginia Setters • John Kennedy • David Corlan • Dr. John Smith • Julie Spence • Glen Strock • Mary Barrett • James "Jim" Magee • Jonathan David Brown • Rocky Green • Annemarié Kleynhans Russouw • Dr. George Umberson

Special Tribute to Floyd McClung Jr.

Floyd McClung Jr. lived his life with a passion for God. I am eternally grateful for his investment in me. He launched me into missions, taught me to be a servant leader, and brought me deep emotional healing. The courage that he and his wife, Sally, demonstrated in their lives and as Floyd faced death will forever be a testimony of their love for God and people. Thank you, God, for my spiritual father, Floyd.

Acknowledgments

My biggest thank you goes to Becky Hefty, my friend and co-writer. My story would not have been written without her talent and hours of work. Becky led me through the process, recruiting many wonderful contributors along the way.

I want to thank Tina Lusby, Addela Bransford, David and Kathy Graham, and Catherine Browning for graciously reading my book in its various stages and helping to make it all it could be through their edits, critiques, and encouragements.

I especially want to acknowledge Barb Foye, who gave generously of her time and skills, fearlessly taking the manuscript apart and giving us the fierce, honest, and accurate critiques and edits we so needed. Thank you, Barb!

Finally, my deep gratitude goes to Scott and Sandi Tompkins, who have a gift for transforming and translating manuscripts into finished products. Thank you both for helping us navigate the publishing process. Above all, thank you for believing enough in my story—God's story—to throw your considerable skill and reputation behind it. God knows how many of his stories are going around the world with your fingerprints on them!

Special Thanks

I want to thank all of the staff and leaders of YWAM Amsterdam, Musicians for Missions, University of the Nations, and YWAM International, with whom I have worked over the years. I've learned so much from so many! Thanks also to the many students who attended our summer programs and UofN schools. I'm glad that many of you became not only lifelong friends of mine, but some of you continue to do awesome things for the Lord. My thanks also go to those who worked so diligently as staff, board members, and advocates at YWAM Santa Fe.

I'm so grateful to those who have mentored me along the way. Some have been pastors, some teachers and elders in the area of music, some peers, and some have been simply Jesus followers who helped teach me more than they'll ever know. All have helped me see myself as Jesus sees me and encouraged me to mentor others.

I've been privileged to know and work with so many fine and dedicated people over the years that I can't begin to name you all individually. You know who you are and how much you have contributed to all the things God has done through the ministry we've shared. My gratitude goes out to all of you. I could not have accomplished what I have without you as coworkers.

I want to thank my family—especially my mother, whom I will thank in heaven someday. It's a blessing to have a family that cares for one another, even those who may not share the same worldview or Christian faith. I know we still share a love that has been deep and binding. And I know you'll be there to share my joys and sorrows as I will be there for you as well.

Above all, I thank my God, who has given me life, love, and healing on this earth and in eternity. May I walk in gratefulness all my life.

Karen Lafferty Discography

Bird in a Golden Sky
Release Date: May 12, 1975
Label: Maranatha! Music, MFM Productions

Sweet Communion
Release Date: June 7, 1978
Label: Maranatha! Music, MFM Productions

Life Pages—Love of the Ages
Release Date: April 20, 1980
Label: Maranatha! Music, MFM Productions

Country to Country
Release Date: February 10, 1982
Label: Maranatha! Music (Asaph Records), MFM Productions

Land of No Goodbyes
Release Date: June 2, 1989
Label: MFM Productions

Hymns from the Heart
Release Date: November 14, 1995
Label: MFM Productions

Multitudes—The Sound of Many Nations
Release Date: September 17, 2003
Label: MFM Productions

Singing My Heart Out—Songs of Worship
Release Date: October 7, 2008
Label: MFM Productions

To purchase CDs, please visit *www.KarenLafferty.com*.

I have lived much more life and have many more stories to tell than I could include in this book. If you are interested in other stories about my growing-up years in New Mexico, life during the Jesus movement, the life of a musicianary, my missions life since returning to New Mexico, or if you would like to see more photos, please visit *KarenLafferty.com/Seek-Ye-First-Book*.

Karen's Music and More Info

All Songs

More Photos and Stories

YouTube—KarenLaffertyMusic

Maranatha Three—Plan of Love

The Praise Album—Seek Ye First

Bird in a Golden Sky

Sweet Communion

Life Pages—Love of the Ages

Country to Country

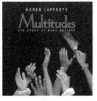

Land of No Goodbyes

Hymns from the Heart

Multitudes—The Sound of Many Nations

Seek Ye First—Singing My Heart Out

Made in the USA
Las Vegas, NV
14 October 2022

57279029R00138